the ART *of* LISTENING PRAYER

the **ART** *of* **LISTENING PRAYER**

SETH BARNES

Ashland Press

Published by Ashland Press.
Ashland Press
6000 Wellspring Trail
Gainesville, GA 30506

ISBN 0-9754305-6-4

Visit Seth Barnes' website at sethbarnes.com.

Printed in the United States of America.

TO KAREN

You've taught me more about listening than anyone
else. During the course of our 24 years of married life, you've
always had the opportunity to tune me out —
I'm thankful that you always listened.

CONTENTS

ACKNOWLEDGMENTS

My mother modeled prayer for my entire life. What a legacy she left me. She was the tangible expression of God's grace.

Along the way, Clint Bokelman has shared an enthusiasm for this subject. His faith in me and in God has kept me going.

Zihna Edwards and Mark Almand have specifically prayed with me for a year about, "What does God want us to do with this manuscript?" Their patience, friendship and commitment have been a gift.

Thanks to Peter Lord. I sat in the audience at a conference of his in 1991 and my world changed. And, thanks to Mike Meyer and Scott Qualls who helped me to find biblical balance along the way. Their refining questions required a year or two of wrestling before coming to a place of peace.

CELEBRATING 10 YEARS

*I*n 2004, when The Art of Listening Prayer was first published, I was experiencing God's disruptive and transformational voice in my own life.

That year, a friend asked me to drop everything I was doing—running a busy short-term missions organization—and partner on a project in Swaziland with him, a tiny country neighboring South Africa with the highest AIDs infection rate in the world.

Is this from you, God, I asked, or just another good opportunity that isn't for me? I fasted and prayed for a week, waiting on the Lord to speak. At the end, I told my friend I was in. I put everything else on hold and left for Swaziland.

And it changed the course of my life.

All the work Adventures in Missions does with 6,000 orphans in Swaziland, as well as my own deeper understanding of discipleship, resulted from that trip, not to mention the World Race.

The question is, did God sound like the suggestion of my friend? Was it the voice of the Lord speaking to me during my time of prayer and fasting? Did he use the Scriptures to convince me?

Ten years of fruit since then tells me that the Lord did show up. But how?

Since then, the art of listening prayer, both this book and the practice it teaches, is as relevant now as it was then.

It is still the cry of so many of our hearts. "Is God someone I can talk to?" I hope that this can be a practical introduction to your conversation. As highlighted in the book, God speaks in a variety of ways. He shows up in our study of Scripture, in the conversations we have with others, or simply through the circumstances of daily life. Other times, he speaks just as you'd speak with a close friend, in a way that feels like a dialogue. You hear something that has the timber and resonance of God's voice in it.

Honestly, I wish I experienced him like that more often.

Since releasing this book ten years ago the Lord has continued to teach me. He has shown me that listening is hard work, whether it's to your wife, your boss, your friends or family. Listening is not something we come to naturally—we have to practice it. It's easy to fall out of practice and spend more time talking than listen.

We need reminders. We need to create space where we can re-focus on listening, where we can hear what God's unending voice is speaking, his love and care for us.

I hope this book will help you do that, and my prayer for you is that you would be able to discover and continue this dialogue for the rest of your life.

Seth Barnes

INTRODUCTION

*T*o me, India during the summer of 2001 might as well have been Mars. I felt so separated from familiar ground. As I walked in the gray, predawn light, the beaches of Bombay began filling up with walkers and joggers and an occasional pack of dogs. Very little of what I saw that morning fit with my experience.

It appeared as though most people were there for exercise, a clearing of the head, and perhaps some conversation with companions.

I observed Hindu temples spaced along the beach. The devout would pause along their route, face the temple, and pray to the gods inside. However, as far as I could tell, none of them either expected or received any answers.

The prayer life of many Christians in America is not unlike that of the devout Hindu on the beaches of Bombay. Yes, we pray to God, not some man-made idol; however, the way in which we pray is surprisingly similar.

Often, our prayers are not like any other normal conversation. For many of us, they are the rote pleadings of children who know well their own needs, but understand little about their Father. Our prayers are the symptoms of shallow, impersonal relationships with Jesus. We expect God to answer through circumstances and events, but never in an actual dialogue.

Most of my life I struggled with the vague notion that God wanted to talk to me and I just wasn't listening hard enough. The God I read about in the Bible regularly interacts not only with mankind, but also with specific men and women. The common denominator I saw in

SETH BARNES

Scripture was that these people who conversed with God were intentional and earnest in their pursuit of a relationship with him. So, I decided to pursue him like that. At the same time I became more aware that he was pursuing me.

While I had talked to God and heard his voice in a variety of ways previously, in 1991 I heard him speak to me in a profoundly personal and unmistakable way. At a time when I most needed to hear it, my Creator told me that he loved me! I don't know that I ever intellectually doubted that, but to hear it from God directly was an overwhelming experience. It changed my life forever–I can't go back!

The two-way communication that is foundational to all relationships is no less important for our relationship with the God who created us to be relational beings. We need to see for ourselves that he wants to talk with us. He wants to put the "personal" back in the personal relationship with Jesus that we tell others we have.

The Next Month

This short devotional aims to add depth to your conversation with God. If your experience interacting with God feels like a monologue, if you hunger for intimacy with God the Father, but feel stuck, unclear as to how to actually go deeper, then perhaps you'll find some answers here.

Over the next month, you'll see that it is possible to converse with God. In fact, you'll see that he invites conversation and expects to regularly interact with us.

Like Esau, many of us trade this birthright for a cheap imitation-stale religion. But there is a way out. The same God who gave us the spirit of adoption, who invites us to call him "Abba Father," gives us the right as his children to talk to him conversationally. Don't you hope against hope that this is true? Aren't you just waiting for someone to show you the way?

There is a way, and it involves the give and take that we expect in any conversation. It requires that we ask God questions and wait for him to respond. Because it involves this process of listening, I call it "listening prayer." It's far more art than science, and practice does help. Over the next month, this devotional will give you help in practicing it. We need to get in the habit of asking God more questions and then expecting his response.

Some of the questions in this devotional will prompt you to seek God for information, and other questions will prompt you to focus on deepening your relationship with him. As you do this, bear in mind that God is far more interested in spending time with you than he is in your diligence in working through a particular assignment. God wants you to seek him with all your heart; he wants your heart more than anything else. Be aware of your natural bent—if you are a more task-oriented person, you may be tempted to focus on informational questions as opposed to relational ones.

What You'll Need

To position yourself to hear the Lord's voice you'll need to find the following:

- Your Bible
- A journal
- Two different colored pens
- A silent room where you can spend at least 45 minutes uninterrupted, more if possible, to quiet yourself for listening prayer. Whether or not

you use it all, the more time you set aside, the better... it's hard to really settle in when you need to watch a clock.

So, begin by asking yourself, "Do I want to hear the Lord's voice enough to make it a priority in my life?"

A Word of Caution

The goal of growing in relationship with God is not easily squeezed into an already tight schedule. If your current pattern is to spend 15 minutes reading down a prayer list just after taking a shower while waiting for the coffee to brew, something else in your schedule is going to need to give. Deep relationships don't happen overnight. This is true for God just as it is for anybody else. If God sees that the pressure of the day is weighing on you and, while waiting for him to speak, in your spirit you are impatiently drumming your fingers on the table, then this devotional may be a waste of your time.

While I suggest setting aside a significant uninterrupted time a day to spend in listening prayer, if this is new to you, you will need to build up to this gradually. It takes practice to focus your mind on him for an extended period of time. Pray and ask him to sweep away the clutter in your mind.

If at the other extreme, you are already desperate to hear the Lord's voice, then don't let your busy life get in the way – you might set aside an hour and a half to move through this devotional at a slower pace. If you're somewhere in the middle, not really there but wanting to grow in the amount of time you spend with God then begin by budgeting 45 minutes the first week and see if you can double it in the weeks that follow. While spending time with someone won't guarantee a close relationship, it will create the space for the relationship to grow. You've got to do a motive check before you begin this process. God says, "You will seek me and find me when you seek me with all your heart."

A Mentor or Coach

A final word of counsel before starting: To get the most out of the next month, you'll need a more experienced partner who can hold you accountable to intentionally invest the time you need to converse with God and to debrief what the Lord is saying to you. Jesus warns us of the blind leading the blind; I encourage you to look for mentors or coaches at least one rung higher on the maturity ladder than yourself when seeking/confirming direction. Pooled ignorance should not be equated with wisdom.

Your coach will ensure that you're investing the time in this and can help you process what God seems to be showing you. Optimally, if your accountability partner has been walking with the Lord for a while, he or she would have the spiritual discernment to help you assess what God may be saying along the way.

Unfortunately, many people don't have anyone in their lives that they can trust with their thoughts and prayers. The idea of writing something down that someone will later review can be intimidating. This is a dilemma you may want to take to the Lord. The advantages of identifying and trusting a coach can be great. It greatly helps to have a sounding board to test the validity of your perceptions as you begin to tune in to the still, small voice of God.

DAY ONE

WHAT IS "LISTENING PRAYER?"

*I*n the winter of 2002 my coworker, Deryck Livingston, and I traveled to Bethel College in Indiana. We were asked by my friend, Professor Terry Linhart, to guest teach his class on discipleship. We felt the Lord asking us to demonstrate that he is alive and that he desires to communicate with us in a personal way. From this, we prepared a lesson that was as interactive as we could make it.

Deryck asked the class, "Who here has never really heard the Lord in a clear way?" A number of hands went up. "Would any of you volunteer to come up here so that we can pray and ask God to speak to you?" One large young man named Ernest came forward to pray with Deryck. They sat at the front of the class while everyone else either prayed or looked on.

Although we believed that the Lord had directed us to go through this exercise, we did so with some trepidation and questioned if anything would happen. The whole exercise required faith. We believed that God wanted to speak to his children, but now we were putting our faith on the line.

Ernest settled into the chair while Deryck laid a hand on his shoulder to pray. It was a simple, sincere prayer.

"Lord, here we are before you. I am sitting here with Ernest who has come forward to hear your voice, to know what you have to say to him. Would you reveal yourself to him as he seeks you now with all his heart?"

We waited in silence. We were expectant and curious, but still a little uncertain. How often do we just stop and wait expectantly on the Lord?

After a while, Deryck quietly asked, "Ernest, have you heard anything? Has God laid anything on your heart?" Ernest nodded and said softly, "He wants me to know how much he loves me."

Deryck paused and then asked, "Can you receive that?" Again Ernest nodded and quietly said with some effort, "I've been trying so hard to do the right thing: to do well in school, to make good choices, to please him." He paused, then said with conviction and wonder, "But he just says he wants me to know he loves me, really loves me, and that all this other stuff doesn't matter that much."

Later, Deryck reflected how everything shifted at that moment. It had been an exercise, a demonstration that God will speak to us if we slow down enough to listen and allow him to speak to us.

"I realized yet again that he is a living God with his own purpose, and here I was setting up a conversation. I suddenly felt awkward, like the time I called my mom to the phone to speak to my dad and lingered a little too long after she picked up. They were talking in a personal way and I got embarrassed. Up there in front of the class with Ernest, I again felt like I was intruding on a very personal, sacred conversation. All of a sudden the room full of people fell away, and I was just with Ernest, encouraging him as he opened up to God. The Lord loves Ernest so much, and he wanted him to know it."

Before he was done, Ernest not only heard God speak, but in his mind also saw a beautiful picture of himself reflecting God's golden light. The change that came over Ernest was visible in his countenance. He was so excited; he finally knew God's love and grace, and was relieved of a burden of performance. What a difference it made for him to know God's love regardless of his efforts! He told us he could do his school-work for the joy of it now and that he wanted to make God smile.

"I need to spend more time like this just being with God. It was so cool just hanging out without trying to think of what to pray about. I realize now that even in prayer I was getting wrapped up in my own concerns. Hey, maybe God doesn't take life so seriously. He might just want me to enjoy life with him."

There were nods and comments of agreement from classmates as Ernest marveled at his experience. But not everyone was convinced.

Ben, another student, said with some consternation, "I don't agree with all this. I think it's contrived. I'm glad Ernest had a good experience, but you can't just tell God what to do and expect him to do it right here, right now. I mean, he's God. We aren't! He speaks to us through his Word and that's enough. Discipleship is training people in allowing him to speak to us through his Word, not through our subjective feelings. Feelings come and go. I don't feel God is here right now, but that doesn't mean I don't believe in him, that I don't have a personal relationship with him. I pray to him and study his Word and live my life in obedience to him and he guides me and loves me. I don't need to hear his voice. He speaks to me through his Word."

We continued with a discussion about the many ways God speaks to us as revealed in Scripture.

Ernest wanted everyone to try it like he did. "It helped me make a breakthrough today on something I have been struggling with all semester. What have you got to lose? I feel like I gained a closer relationship with God. I mean, I can talk to him about anything right now and I think he would respond. It's so simple, and yet here I am in a Christian college, taking a class on Discipleship, and I'm just realizing the difference between talking about listening to God and really listening. It's so simple, it's stupid! We waste so much time trying to please God and do the right thing, and maybe he doesn't even really want that. Maybe he just wants to hang out with us and love on us. Wow! What a concept!"

Skeptics like Ben

If at this point if you identify more with Ben than Ernest, welcome to the party. Growing up in America isn't easy; we're a nation of skeptics. It's easier to take potshots at something than it is to embrace it. We've been disappointed so many times, seen so many promises come to nothing. Every day we hear new stories of some getting duped. And in our own lives, we've prayed a hundred times for something and perhaps we've felt like God never reached down out of heaven to answer us.

The idea that God speaks to humans, that in fact he may be speaking to you this very day, may seem to contradict your experience. It's a wonder anybody is willing to consider the possibility! If you're a skeptic, you're in good company. But if you're honest, you may begin to admit a couple of things.

First, wouldn't you want to be able to talk with your creator and hear him talking back? Wouldn't that be the most wonderful thing imaginable? Don't you hope against hope that it's possible? Second, this "personal relationship with God" that we as a Church advertise to nonbelievers may not feel very personal at all.

Somewhere along the line you may feel as though you've been sold a bill of goods. We're so saturated with doctrine that has little or no basis in our experience that we look and act like hypocrites. It's time you face the issue; trifling with God doesn't serve him – if our friends can see the unreality of our faith, then he certainly can.

So what if you could set your skepticism aside for a month and try listening for God, just like Moses did? Or Samuel, or David, or the disciples, or Paul, or many of Christendom's greatest saints did down through history?

What if they understood something that you've missed? Also, what if God was just waiting to break out of the box you've had him in, to show you that he does still talk to people and wants to talk to you? You may not be that far away from it even now. Chances are you already do hear the Lord's voice and just struggle to admit it.

You may find yourself in the position of the woman who, when reflecting on her journey of faith said, "God used so many people to reach me over the years. Each time it seemed like God was saying, 'I'm still here.' It was obvious that running into these people was not a coincidence."

Well, if it was as obvious as she says, then why doesn't she just go ahead and give God credit for what he was saying through all those people? Why was she (and why are we all) so tentative in crediting God when he speaks?

Maybe God has been talking like that to a lot of us, but we're just not listening. We don't know how to listen. When he speaks, we say, "It's almost as if he were speaking." We don't want to dishonor him by attributing words to him that he never uttered. But we never consider the disrespect of appearing deaf before the Almighty.

God has said in Scripture that he loves faith, that without faith you cannot please him (Hebrews 11:6). He implores us over and over to seek him. Why not take a risk and begin searching for the still, small voice of God that may be speaking to you, even today?

The Process

The fact is, God does speak to you, and he uses a variety of means to do so. As you begin listening to God and hearing his voice, you may find that a question posed in the devotional will lead you to ask the Lord one of your own. That's great! The purpose of this devotional is not to keep you dependent on it, but that at some point, your conversation with God will begin to flow naturally. You may find that the Lord begins to guide your conversations more over time. Again, the goal is for you to grow in your personal relationship with God, not to complete every question.

Getting Started

Begin in silence. Ask the Lord to speak to you by showing you your heart. For instance, what are your motives in going through this devotional? Write this initial question in your journal, and then listen for God's response. Ask for his protection.

Next, ask the Lord a question and wait for his reply in faith. Remember James 1:5-7: "If any of you lacks wisdom, he should ask God." When you receive an impression of what the Lord may be saying, write it down. Use these questions as a conversation starter and then continue talking with him on your own – it's what he's been waiting for!

The Listening Prayer Process

1. When you are ready, quiet yourself and examine your heart. It's often good to begin by reading Scripture. Ask the Lord to speak to you through it.

2. Ask the Lord to protect you in Jesus' name from deception.

3. Ask him to speak clearly in a way that you can understand, and to confirm anything he shared with you in Scripture.

4. Next, write down your questions for prayer.

5. Then pause. This is where you wait and listen. The Lord has much to say to you. He may direct you to another passage of Scripture. He may share a tender word. Whatever you feel he may be saying to you, write it down.

Each day after the reading, questions are listed. You may want to "make them your own" by transferring them to your journal. Or, you may want to write in the brief space provided there.

We will talk more about the journaling process tomorrow. For now, let me share a simple and helpful method. In a quiet room with your Bible(s) and journal, take two different colored ink pens. Use the first ink color to record your own thoughts. You'll use the second pen to record what you sense God is saying. The different colored inks clarify "who's talking." I use a black pen to record my prayers. If the Lord responds to a question I've asked, I journal this in blue ink.

This process of listening may feel awkward and, possibly, presumptuous. It contains the potential for mistaking ordinary thoughts for the voice of God. But the important thing is that you are giving God the opportunity to speak to you. Just as children must be taught to listen and to sit respectfully during adult conversation, so we must learn to stop our one-way monologues with our heavenly Father.

If you are like most people, you'll find that stray thoughts of things–to–do flash on the screen of your mind. You may find it helpful to have a separate piece of paper on which to write TO DO list items. In fact, that's often how I get direction for my day. But press on beyond your daily tasks to engage the Lord in listening prayer.

Questions to Ask the Lord

Spend some time in prayer. Ask the Lord the questions below. Don't worry about missing God—this is just practice in "tuning in" to his still, small voice. Rely on the Bible to help you sift any stray notions. Later your coach can help you look at this in light of Scripture. It may be uncomfortable at first but, as you wait, gradually that discomfort will be replaced by impressions of what he's communicating to you. He is a gentle and good Shepherd; trust him to speak to you.

1. Are there ways in which I have offended you?

2. What can I do to keep from offending you in the future?

3. Is there anything you'd like to share with me?

DAY TWO

HOW TO BEGIN YOUR JOURNAL

*L*ast Fall, I was looking for God's help in the way that I led our ministry organization (Adventures In Missions). As a whole, we needed to connect with him, so I began to journal my prayers. Here are two examples of my prayers and God's responses from that journal:

> 9/27—Lord, drill down with us. Show us yourself. Meet us in our times of worship and in our times of ministry. Is there anything you want to say to our group?
>
> Philippians 3:13-14: "Forgetting what is behind and straining toward what is ahead, I press on toward the goal to win the prize..."
>
> Wait for what I will show you.
>
> Philippians 2:2: Be "like-minded, having the same love, being one in spirit and purpose."
> ...
> *10/28—Thanks for a good weekend. I confess my own inadequacy. I'm caught up in my own agenda. And I continually struggle to discern your will and leading.*
>
> *Walk on the paths of righteousness. Minister to others. Seek first my Kingdom. Rest in my love. I will accomplish my purposes.*

After I wrote down these short prayers and sensed

the Lord responding to me, I noticed that two things had happened, both of which encouraged me.

First, I had a specific answer to a specific question. The demands of leadership can be great at times. As the leader of our ministry, I needed to be able to share my perception of what God is saying to our team on that day, not eat the crumbs of yesterday's manna from heaven.

A second thing that happened generally happens whenever I hear God speak. In communicating with me, God reaffirmed our relationship. When I go through a dry spell in hearing from God – which happens – I begin to doubt that he even wants to have a conversation with me. When he breaks through that period of silence, he almost doesn't need to say anything of any consequence at all. The mere possibility that the almighty Creator is speaking to me is overwhelming!

Using A Journal

If you've never heard God, then everything you've read so far probably sounds like a theological treatise. There is a huge difference between seeing the moon and walking on its surface. The Bible says, "For God so loved the world..." (John 3:16), but you need to see for yourself that God cares, and that he cares about you. You need the experience of listening for and hearing his voice for yourself.

The good news is that he is eager to talk with you. Scripture says, "Anyone who comes to him must believe that he exists and that he rewards those who earnestly seek him" (Hebrews 11:6). Sometimes we just need a tool to help us focus. Because our minds are cluttered, we need help to focus when we obscure the Lord's voice. A tool that many have found helpful is a journal.

Writing down our prayers helps in two ways:
- It helps us focus.
- It creates a record to compare with experience.

By journaling our prayers and our impressions of God's answers, we fine-tune our spiritual ears to better hear him. Writing our impression of the Lord's response creates in us an expectancy that he will respond. In effect, we stir up the very faith without which it is impossible to please him.

Regularly "tuning into" the Lord's voice builds the habit patterns of submission and expectancy that are necessary for the exercise of spiritual gifts. For example, you may sense the Lord wanting to use you to encourage someone. However, unless you look for the specific opportunity to use your gift of exhortation, nothing happens.

For example, anyone who believes the Bible is God's inerrant word will agree that it is the Holy Spirit's job to convict us of sin (John 16:8). Let's imagine that you say something mean about your friend Rachel. Subsequently, you hear the Holy Spirit whisper in your mind, "You shouldn't have said that about Rachel. You should apologize." You then have the opportunity to dismiss this thought by saying, "No, that's too much trouble." Or you may respond in obedience.

This kind of limited dialogue is normal. It happens every day in the lives of most Christians. To bring focus to your dialogue by journaling is an age-old Christian discipline. To note in your journal, "I hear the Holy Spirit saying: 'You should apologize to Rachel,'" is hardly a heretical activity. The Holy Spirit's job is to convict us of sin; that conviction typically comes to us as a thought, "You shouldn't have done that."

Apply It

Sometimes all we hear from God is silence – notice how this generally happens when we have previously ignored him by willfully going our own way. This creates distance and can get in the way of listening prayer. In other words, our sin can quench the Spirit. But, if we open ourselves up to him, he will show us how we can be restored in our personal relationship. The Holy Spirit speaks to us about our sin not to condemn us, but to help us draw near to him.

We'll make this process concrete when we get to the prayer time at the end of today's devotional. You'll begin your time with the Lord by saying, "Please show me anything that has put distance between us."

Next, wait to see if God brings anything to mind. If he does, take your second pen and write down in your journal what he shows you.

After this, take up your other pen and write a prayer of repentance to him. If you felt the prompting of the Spirit and recorded it, you've begun a dialogue with him!

This is the first baby step in developing a conversational relationship with the Lord. You can always take your conversation with God to another level. Using this devotional, you'll begin to journal your prayers to God using this same method.

How Do We Know it's God?

How do we avoid mistaking our own thoughts for God's? Obviously, our first check it to see if it lines up with Scripture. Use the questions in the box on the next page to clarify if God has spoken.

To get perspective, I suggest that you sharpen your skills of discernment by regularly submitting your journal for review to a spiritual authority to who you're accountable. By reading and praying over your journal once a week, this person can help you distinguish those thoughts that are random and self-generated from the times when God speaks to you.

1 Thessalonians 5:21 says, "Test all things; hold fast what is good." But how do we do this?

Ask the Following Questions to Clarify if God Has Spoken:

• Was it a clear word or just an impression? God may give us different degrees of confidence in what he has said. We therefore need to humbly admit our fallibility.
• Does it exalt Christ? (John 16:14)
• Is it Scriptural? Scripture is our authority. God does not contradict himself (Proverbs 30:5-6).
• Do other Christians confirm it? (Proverbs 20:18, Proverbs 15:22)
• Will it produce good fruit? (John 15:1-16)
• Will it produce spiritual growth? (John 11:41-42, Isaiah 55:10)
• Does God cause it to actually take place? (Isaiah 55:11, Deuteronomy 18:21-22)

After you've clarified whether God has spoken, you must be very careful with what he has said. Is your understanding of his meaning accurate? The actual words God has spoken to your heart may be accurate, but your interpretation may be incorrect. Distinguish between the two.

In addition, be sure to ask, "What is the application?" or, "So, what now?" The word and the interpretation may be correct, but misapplied. Therefore, we may "miss" God at any of three critical steps:

1. Hearing what he said
2. Interpreting it
3. Applying it to our lives

Scripture Meditation

Spend a minute or more just thinking about the following passage: "Should not a people inquire of their God?" (Isaiah 8:19)

Pray

"Lord, do you expect me to inquire of you? Do you expect that of my church? What do you want to teach me from this passage?" Wait in silence as the Holy Spirit reveals truth to you.

> 1. Is there anything that has put distance between us?
> 2. Have I treated you as less than a friend?
> 3. My own prayer of repentance:

Think for a moment about fresh, white snow. Really think about it. Know that when you have sought God's forgiveness, he has forgiven you (Isaiah 1:18, Psalm 51:7). In his eyes, you are just as pure and white as that fresh, new fallen snow. Is there something you struggle to forgive yourself for? Go before God with it, and ask him to speak the truth to you about it.

DAY THREE

IS OUR PERSONAL RELATIONSHIP WITH JESUS *REALLY* PERSONAL?

I first met my wife in 1978, both of us juniors at Wheaton College. It did not take long during the course of our relationship to know that she was the one for me. Yet, I faced a couple of problems. I didn't really know her, and worse, she was engaged to another man!

Those were dark days. All I knew was that I had to get to know this stranger who had captured my heart. I schemed and plotted. Who were her friends? What classes did she take? Where did she study? I was desperate to get to know her, yet I couldn't appear to be overeager in the process, lest I scare her off.

Fortunately for me, her best friend liked one of my best friends. Soon enough, we found ourselves sitting at the same table in the library studying. Concentrating was nearly impossible for me. I was infatuated.

Now 25 years later, I know so much more about Karen! We've lived on exotic tropical islands, made homes in four different towns in America, and raised five children together. I know how she likes her coffee in the morning and that I shouldn't talk to her until she's had it. I know all about her friends and what her silences mean. We hide nothing from one another.

What a difference spending time together makes! Needless to say, our relationship has become personal. My initial infatuation cannot be compared to the fruit of a life I've lived walking alongside Karen. If I continue to pay attention, I can still learn new things about her every week.

It's the same way in our relationship with God. As

we grow in intimacy, we share our heart with him and as he shares more of his heart with us. The infatuation phase merely lasts for a season as we seek to know more of him every day.

Jesus Wants A Personal Relationship

Jesus wants us not to only know about him, but to actually have a deep, personal relationship with him—to know him and to be known by him. John 17:3 says, "Now this is eternal life: that they may know you, the only true God, and Jesus Christ, whom you have sent."

By looking at the Greek origin of the word "know" or "knowing," it is translated to mean the 'most intimate of relationships'. By this, you can see that God wants our relationship with him to be a deep and intimate.

Jesus makes clear how important it is that we know him when he clarifies the penalty for not knowing him in Matthew 7:23, "Then I will tell them plainly, 'I never knew you. Away from me, you evildoers!'"

This 'knowing' that Jesus describes is the same kind of knowing we see him talking about in John 10:27: "My sheep listen to my voice; I know them..."

As evangelical Christians, we claim to have a personal relationship with Jesus Christ. Yet how many of us actually walk in relationship with him that is personal? Relationships involve give and take, mutual interaction and dialogue. Marriages that lack this kind of interaction can grow stale.

For example, if I relate to my wife by giving her a daily list of things to do, or by telling her about my thoughts, never asking her what her thoughts or feelings are, then my relationship with her will be impersonal. I will know little about her and she will not know that I care about her. To have a personal relationship with my wife, I must listen to her as well as speak.

Our relationship with God should work in the same way. Jeremiah 33:3 says, "Call to me and I will answer you..."

God wants us to give him our praises, our struggles, and our questions. In return, he also wants to give to us his counsel, encouragement, and consolation. This interaction becomes the fabric of our relationship. The more frequent and honest our give-and-take with Jesus, the more personal it becomes.

What else can we say about this relationship?

We know that in Genesis 1:27, it says that God created us in his image. We also know that Jesus became a man. Therefore, we serve a God who is personal—not a book, or a statue, or a vapor, or a religion.

Psalm 139:1-2 says, "O Lord, you have searched me and you know me... you perceive my thoughts from afar." God created us, so he obviously knows everything about us!

We also know that we were created to be in relationship with God. Because we are created in God's image, it's not unreasonable to think that we might apply the same relational principles to our interactions with him that we do in our other relationships.

This can be understandably uncomfortable.

God may be personal, but he is also different from us in some critical ways. He is invisible, all-powerful, and completely holy. He does not typically speak in an audible voice. He is transcendent, or in other words, he is far above our understanding.

So while we may look for give-and-take in our relationship with Jesus, oftentimes the main thing we hear is silence. It is no wonder Christians struggle to make their relationship with him a truly personal one. Silence in conversation usually feels awkward.

While it's true that God tells us over and over in his word to seek him and to love him, we must suspend our expectations of how he will respond to us. As we seek to know God personally, we must not lose sight of his transcendence.

Scripture Meditation

Spend a minute or more just thinking about the following passages: "He calls his own sheep by name and leads them out. When he has brought out all his own, he goes on ahead of them, and his sheep follow him because they know his voice" (John 10:3-4).

"I am the good shepherd; I know my sheep and my sheep know me..." (John10:14).

Pray

"Lord, show me what you want me to learn from this passage." Wait in silence as the Holy Spirit reveals truth to you.

Questions To Ask The Lord

1. God, is my walk with you really personal? When has it been most personal?

2. Do I really understand how to have a personal relationship? What makes a relationship with you personal?

3. How do I hear your voice?

4. Do I possess a hunger for a closer walk with you? What would an increased hunger for a closer walk with you look like?

5. Where do I start? How can I begin to grow more in my walk with you?

Imagine going out for a cup of coffee with God. If he were one of your best friends, what would you want to tell him? Tell Jesus those things. If you would ask your friend questions, you can ask Jesus!

"Today, if you hear his voice, do not harden your hearts..." (Psalm 95:7-8)

DAY FOUR

GOD WANTS TO RELATE TO US

*T*his story comes from Katie Moss, a missionary to Uganda. She relates how God called her there:

"I thought I was hearing God wrong, because there seemed so many good reasons to stay, but it was that still, small voice that just kept saying, "Go." So I packed my bags and left all that was comfortable to go to a foreign land that he would show me. I was scared, sad, and totally alone.

When I arrived, I asked the Lord to reveal my purpose here. I mean, there were plenty of opportunities for ministry, but nothing was filling the void in my heart.

Then last night I went for coffee with one of the ladies in the village here. Her name is Olga. She is 24 years old and loves the Lord. We have been doing some ministry together at the university here in Kampala and she has been someone good for me to talk to and pray with. When we sat down, we prayed that the Lord would have his way in our time and that he would be glorified. Let me say this—I felt the Holy Spirit fall, and it wasn't like a dove. He came in a way that we couldn't help but feel his presence. Olga began to weep and share her story with me.

Olga comes from a family of non-believers that strongly persecute Christians. She has seven brothers and sisters, one of her sisters being a Christian. Her dad kicked her sister out of the house when he found out she had decided to follow Jesus. Her sister has since strayed from the Lord and Olga hasn't heard from her in months.

Olga's parents have a horrible marriage; her dad is abusive and unfaithful and her mom is about to have a nervous breakdown. They are even on the verge of kicking Olga out because she is not stepping down from what she believes.

Olga said that for almost a year she has been praying that God would send her help, someone who knows how to pray for her and her family, someone who understands the pain of where she is. He has heard her cry. To the same degree I know I am saved, I know that God sent me here for her. Only God would strip me from my family to come and minister to someone else's. What a testimony of his love for her, that he would send someone 6,000 miles just to say, "I heard you and I love you.'"

A Theme in Scripture

All throughout Scripture, we see a picture of God in pursuit of people. He's romancing us. He wants one thing: people who will love him with their whole heart. This is why we see him in the Old Testament as a jealous God. Over and over in Scripture, we see the theme of God wooing his people. The Israelites responded by structuring their lives around him, following his laws, and setting aside time to worship him. The New Testament example is even more extreme. Ministry and discipleship were not just tasks on the disciple's to-do list—they were as natural as eating and drinking. This is the kind of undiluted devotion that God desires from us.

Apply It

Trace the theme of the undivided heart through Scripture and you see what God is after. He wants a whole-hearted relationship with us.

- Exodus 20:3: "You shall have no other gods before me."
- Matthew 22:37: Jesus restates: "Love the Lord your God with all your heart..."
- In Deuteronomy, we are encouraged at least 10 times to love him with all our hearts."
- The Psalms paints a story of God wooing our hearts. And of people responding: Psalm 119:58: "I have sought you with all my heart.
- Psalm 51:17: "A broken and contrite heart, O God, you will not despise."
- Psalm 86:11: "Give me an undivided heart."
- Proverbs 23:26: "My son, give me your heart."
- Jeremiah 29:13: "You will seek me and find me when you seek me with all your heart."
- Ezekiel 11:19: "I will give them an undivided heart."
- Joel 2:12: "Return to me with all your heart."
- Matthew 5:8: "Blessed are the pure in heart."
- 2 Timothy 2:2: "Call on the Lord out of a pure heart."

Scripture Meditation

Spend a minute or more just thinking about the following passage: "I have sought you with all my heart" (Psalm 119:58).

Pray

"Lord, show me what you want me to learn from this passage." Wait in silence as the Holy Spirit reveals truth to you. Take the time to write down what you hear from God.

Questions to Ask the Lord

Take some time to write a love letter to your heavenly Father. Have you expressed to him the deepest yearnings of your heart lately? Have you thanked him for all he has given you?

After you have written for a while, pause and wait. In the ensuing silence, God may want to share something of his own heart for you.

DAY FIVE

GOD WANTS TO RELATE TO US AS A FATHER

*M*any fathers struggle to communicate with their teenagers. My own dad still jokes about when I became a teenager, I withdrew into my room in the basement only to emerge five years later in time to go off to college. We struggled to connect; I was confused and depressed. My communication skills were lacking and I was more comfortable behind a book.

Those teenage years were painful ones for me. I frequently felt isolated and misunderstood. Dad and I lived in the same house, but we were distant. Someone needed to take me by the hand and show me how to interact with people.

Some years later, my dad called and asked if I wanted to go on a kayaking trip with him. We paddled down jungle rivers lined with moss-laden trees. We saw anteaters and crocodiles. Eventually the river dumped into the open, azure ocean. The weather was perfect, and the beaches along the way were white.

In retrospect, I see that it was an invitation to get to know him as more than a father – to know him as a friend. We set aside the awkward memories of my adolescence and had the best time we ever had together. It was a breakthrough in our relationship. I got to know my dad in a deeper way as we finally learned to communicate.

What is it that makes the role of a father so important in our lives?

While much of what we might say holds true for mothers as well, the role of a father is irreplaceable. Perhaps it's the fact that when we're young, we start out so small and defenseless. We need the protection that fathers provide. We can't even feed ourselves as we start out on life's journey. Parents not only get food for us, they put it in our mouths. They nurture us in a hundred different ways. As we grow in awareness, they explain how the world works. They help us acquire the skills with which we navigate life. Because they constantly help us develop, we look to them for approval.

A son may ask as he learns to hammer a nail for the first time, "Is this how I do it, Dad?" Or a daughter may ask her father before the first day of school, "Does this outfit look good?" If he smiles with an enthusiastic "Yes!" then she's good to go. Without a father's approval, there would be much more trial and error in our lives.

In the big scope of things, we are constantly adjusting ourselves as we grow up—our skills and image—to better fit the requirements of the world in which we live. This adjustment mechanism is the asking for and receiving of approval. Fathers who withhold approval from their children are sure to foster their insecurity. Children who withhold respect for their fathers are breaking one of God's commandments.

Apply It

God not only wants a relationship with us, he wants to relate to us as a father. When asked by his disciples how they should pray, Jesus said they should address God as 'Father.' Jesus himself modeled this relationship, frequently referring to God as 'my Father'. When Jesus began his ministry, God voiced his approval, "This is my Son, whom I love; with him I am well pleased" (Matthew 3:17).

As our heavenly Father, God acts as our protector, our provider, our friend, our confidante, and our teacher. He has much to show us and already loves us without condition. There is nothing we can do to win his approval; we already have it.

Scripture Meditation

Spend a minute or more just thinking about the following passage: "Because you are sons, God sent the Spirit of his Son into our hearts, the Spirit who calls out, 'Abba, Father'" (Galatians 4:6).

Pray

"Heavenly Father, I want to look to you for your approval. I know that you love all your children, but I confess that I struggle sometimes to feel that love and to see you as a Father. My own father let me down sometimes. But you have said that you'd never leave me or forsake me. You've promised to guide and protect me. These are truths that I believe with my mind. But today I'd like to feel your care for me in the depths of my heart. Would you tell me today how you feel about me?"

Wait on the Lord in silence.

Questions to Ask the Lord

Spend some time in prayer. Get completely alone and distraction-free, so you can listen closely. Ask the Lord the questions below.

1. Heavenly Father, would you show me any ways in which my relationship with my earthly father has colored my perception of you?

2. Is there anything I need to change to relate to you more as my Father? What is it?

3. What are some ways that you've related to me in the past as Father?

4. Are there ways in which I can better honor you as my heavenly Father? Would you show them to me?

Sometimes our past relationship with our father hinders our relationship to God. Maybe you didn't feel that your real father understood you. Maybe he didn't take time to listen to you. Maybe he didn't tell you he loved you. Maybe he even hurt you. But God isn't like that. He is a perfect father. Think about what that all means. Consciously make an effort to see him as different from your earthly father. Give him the chance to listen to you and then see what he has to say to you.

DAY SIX

HOW DOES OUR HEAVENLY
FATHER COMMUNICATE?

Our youngest daughter's learning disability resulted in social issues that have left my wife and I with a perplexing question. How could we help Leah to engage socially? What could we do that would draw her out of her shell?

One day, God gave Karen the answer: a dog. However, we already had a farm dog living outside. Karen, on the other hand, had a small, cuddly indoor dog in mind. And so the search began!

Considerable research pointed in the direction of a cockapoo – a half cocker spaniel, half poodle. So we started looking for cockapoos on the internet, in the paper, and asked around to some of our friends.

A friend in South Carolina finally called and said, "I know just the dog! Some friends of ours have a half poodle, half Maltese puppy. They are usually gone all day and the puppy is starving for affection—so they want to give it away."

Immediately, Karen and Leah drove to South Carolina and fell in love with this little fur ball at first sight. "Whimsy" turned out to be a bundle of affection and constant source of amusement. At just over seven pounds, he was more fur than anything else.

Leah now has responsibility for feeding, washing, and walking Whimsy. Early on, Leah began to regularly boss him around and he slowly began to develop a routine comprised of just three activities: sleep on Leah's lap, eat, or play. Though he spends most of his time sleeping, occasionally he grabs a dog toy and starts running around the house. It's his way of saying, "I want to play!"

What a bundle of energy Whimsy is to watch when he's playing! The name fits perfectly as every playful burst seems whimsical in origin. Whether darting about the house, chasing imaginary rabbits, playing keep-away with the ball, or any manner of games, Whimsy quickly found his way into all of our hearts. He was just what the doctor ordered and has continually been a tangible demonstration of God's care for Leah.

I have many ways of communicating with Whimsy. If I spill food on the floor, all I have to do is tap my foot and he runs over to lick it up. If he's done something wrong, the tone of my voice says plenty—I don't need words to communicate displeasure. If I grab the leash, it's time for a walk. When I am packing suitcases, Whimsy gets a sense of insecurity and fear of getting left behind.

I would never want to restrict the ways in which I can communicate with Whimsy. Words are just a small part of my repertoire.

Similarly, why should God (who is infinitely creative) limit himself? The list of the methods he has used in the Bible shows us something about him, but it doesn't begin to do justice to the possibilities available to him. The God who has communicated to people in so many ways throughout history wants to have a conversation with us. We need to be open about what shape that conversation takes, allowing the Lord to choose his means of communication.

Apply It

Scripture shows that God uses a variety of methods to communicate to his people. The following is a list of some of the methods he has used. As you go through the list, find the Scriptures in your Bible. To properly interpret Scripture, we need to look at the context.

A Warning

Though God has spoken to people in the past in certain ways, it doesn't mean he will necessarily do so with us. Some people cite these examples and state that we can expect God to speak in this way to us. This boxes God in.

These examples show us the patterns of a God who wants to communicate with people and will not be limited in how he does so. Ask God to speak to you through what you read and note the patterns.

Through Scripture

- Acts 2:16-21 "This is what was spoken by the prophet Joel..." Peter links the manifestations of the Holy Spirit with Old Testament prophecy.
- Acts 4:25-26 "You spoke by the Holy Spirit through the mouth of your servant, our father David." Peter and John echo Psalm 2 in their prayer.

Through Others

- Deuteronomy 18:17-19 "I will put my words in his mouth." God declares that he will speak through a prophet.

- Numbers 15:2 "Speak to the Israelites." God commands Moses to communicate his desires to his people.

• Isaiah 28:11 "With foreign lips and strange tongues God will speak to this people." A prophecy to the Israelites.

Through Circumstances/Events

• Genesis 50:20 Joseph said, "You intended to harm me, but God intended it for good." Joseph tells his brothers how God redeemed his bad circumstances.
• Acts 1:26 "They cast lots." After days of praying, with no obvious direction, they ask God to use the luck of the draw to decide who will replace Judas.

Impressions

• Acts 15:36 A desire to make a return visit. Paul suggests to Barnabas that they go visit the churches they had planted.
• 1 Corinthians 12:7-9 Gifts often originate as impressions from the Lord. Wisdom, knowledge, and faith all start out as Holy Spirit-generated thoughts.

Audibly

• 1 Samuel 3:7-10 "The Lord called Samuel... Samuel said, 'Speak for your servant is listening.'" Eli guides Samuel after having never heard the Lord's voice.
• Exodus 33:11 "The Lord would speak to Moses face to face, as a man speaks with his friend." Moses, having spent 40 years in the desert and having confronted Pharaoh, converses with God.

• 1 Kings 19:11-12 "And after the fire came a gentle whisper." Elijah finds God not in the wind, an earthquake, or a fire, but a whisper.

Inwardly

• 1 Samuel 23:2 "he inquired of the Lord...The Lord answered." David hears of the Philistines' attack and looting and asks God what his response should be.

Through Surprising Means

• Exodus 3:4 A bush. Of all things, God speaks to Moses out of a shrub.

Through Visions

• Ezekiel 12:23-28 "Every vision will be fulfilled." God is tired of cynicism concerning his speaking. Though there have been false visions, he promises a change.
• Ezekiel 40:2-4 "Tell...everything you see." Ezekiel had many visions that God asked him to record.
• Daniel 8:1 "I, Daniel, had a vision." Daniel actually has a series of visions that leave him exhausted and ill.

Through Dreams

• Genesis 37:5 "Joseph had a dream." Joseph tells his dream to his brothers and they hate him all the more.

Through Demonstrations of Power

• Acts 3:1-10: "All the people were... filled with wonder and amazement." Peter and John heal a beggar, draw a crowd, and bring thousands to Christ.
• 1 Corinthians 2:4-5 "My message and my preaching were not with wise and persuasive words, but with a demonstration of the Spirit's power." Paul recounts his evangelistic methodology – it's not his words that count, but what God does through him that communicates most loudly.

Scripture Meditation

Spend a minute or more just thinking about the following passage: "David inquired of God...God answered him." (1 Chronicles 14:14 -16)

Pray

"Heavenly Father, where did David get this habit of asking you questions? Why is it that you want us to ask you questions? What do you want to show me about this

Scripture?" Wait in silence as the Holy Spirit reveals truth to you.

Questions to Ask the Lord

1. What are some ways in which you have spoken to me in the past?

2. How have I quenched your Spirit when you wanted to speak to me?

3. Is there anything I'm doing now that is quenching your Spirit?

4. Have I limited the ways in which you've desired to speak? How?

5. What can I do to better hear your voice?

Go outside somewhere in nature and imagine sitting with God. As you look at the world around you, ask God to teach you about his love. Can you see God's love as you look at trees, hills, water or wildlife that you may find around you?

DAY SEVEN

GOD'S COMMUNICATION PRINCIPLES

*T*he hospitality of our host families during the mission trip I led to England in 2003 was overwhelming. There were so many people who wanted to house our team that each evening we had the privilege of eating at different homes, splitting up into teams for tea and dinner.

On one particular evening, one of the teams forgot to get the address of the home they were invited to. However, they had the family name and the street circled on a map. Not knowing which house to knock on when they arrived, they began to pray.

Then they ran into a woman on the street. "Do you know where the Ellis family lives?" they asked her.

"Sure, they live right over there." The team went over to the house, rang the doorbell and waited. A confused looking man opened the door.

"Are you Mr. Ellis?" they asked.

"Yes I am," he replied. "Well, we're here for dinner."

"Oh, right. OK, fine, well come on in then. I'll call my wife, she isn't here now." They went inside and sat down while Mr. Ellis got them Cokes.

A few minutes later, Mrs. Ellis came rushing in and frantically began cleaning and straightening the house all the while saying, "I'm sorry, I don't know how this happened, we didn't realize you were coming here right now, but I'll get some leftovers out of the fridge and we'll be eating in no time at all!"

The team ended up having a wonderful time with the Ellis family. They were so sweet and funny.

When the team arrived at its next venue, the

leaders looked concerned. "Why didn't you eat with the Ellis'?" they asked. "They just called and had a wonderful meal ready for you, and you never showed up!"

"We did eat with the Ellis'!" the team said.

It turned out that Mr. Ellis's brother – also a Mr. Ellis – lived in the same area. So when complete strangers arrived unannounced on their doorstep expecting to be given dinner, these good folks invited them in and fed them! Now that's hospitality.

Some Principles

Communication can be complicated and can complicate our relationships. We've established that God wants a personal relationship and that he uses a variety of means to communicate.

This book is founded on the premise that his relationship with us is similar to our other relationships in that it involves frequent two-way communication. In John 15:15, Jesus says to his disciples, "I have called you friends." John 10 then describes this personal relationship as one between a shepherd and his sheep. It is a relationship in which the shepherd calls to the sheep, and the sheep obey him. Therefore, in a relationship, whether friends or acquaintances, talking must happen.

Looking at Scripture, we know a few divine communication principles that describe the way God wants us to interact with him: Asking questions, expecting a response, focusing on attention, recognizing his voice, knowing there is variety in communication, expressing affection, and honesty.

1. Ask Questions

In normal personal relationships, dialogue is initiated by asking questions. Questions prompt responses.

The Scriptures are full of examples of people asking God questions. Isaiah 8:19 it says, "Should not a people inquire of their God?" Also, Jeremiah 10:21 says, "The shepherds are senseless and do not inquire of the Lord; so they do not prosper." Further, in Matthew 7:7 it says, "Ask and it will be given to you." God wants to answer your questions. He expects us to initiate dialogue, just as we would in any personal relationship.

2. Expect A Response

In normal personal relationships, after posing a question, it is customary to expect a response and to wait for it. So it is with God.

He is neither rude nor unreasonable. He wants to answer us; he doesn't want to exasperate us. Matthew 7:9 says, "Which of you, if his son asks for bread, will give him a stone?" Then in Jeremiah 33:3 it says he will answer us if we call on him. Habakkuk 2:1 underscores this principle as well.

We often lack faith or patience after posing a question to wait for God's response. Or we doubt that he will answer us (see James 1:5-8).

3. Focus On His Attention

In normal personal relationships, the listener does not interrupt or allow distractions, but focuses his attention on the speaker.

Psalm 46:10 says, "Be still and know that I am God." Being still in this sense means more than physical inactivity—it implies a stillness of mind and spirit. Yet in our conversations with God, we often allow irrelevant thoughts or outside distractions to interrupt us. Often we are like rude children who have never been taught to sit still and focus our attention on what others are saying. In the process, we can shut down our dialogue. We allow our own thoughts to run ahead of and get in the way of God's answer to our question.

It's important to intentionally quiet ourselves. We need to be free from distractions. Matthew 6:6 says that when we pray, we should "close the door." The place of prayer should be private and distraction-free.

How can we hear his still, small voice if our own thoughts are running rampant? In John 10:27, Jesus says, "My sheep listen to my voice." He says this multiple times, emphasizing its importance.

4. Recognize His Voice

In normal personal relationships we recognize the voice of the other party. While our lives are filled with hundreds of relationships, we recognize the voices of our friends. They can call us on the phone, and we can identify them before they give their name. John 10:4 says, "His sheep follow him because they know his voice."

Author Peter Lord tells the story of an entomologist studying crickets who could distinguish the unique sounds of over 200 crickets. He did this by listening carefully to them over a period of time. Gradually, he began to recognize their differences.

I have a pilot friend who can distinguish the sounds of different jets flying five miles overhead in the same way. So it is as we listen to God's voice.

The point is, if you are not accustomed to hearing God's voice, don't expect miracles right away. Keep practicing. Just as you learned to recognize the voice of a friend, you will learn to recognize his voice.

5. Variety in Communication

In normal personal relationships, people use a variety of means to communicate. I write letters, send e-mails, make phone calls, communicate messages through others, and talk to my wife, Karen.

In all these different means of communication, she has learned not to look at the channel (the means I use to communicate), but at the message being conveyed. This principle fits with the variety of methods we see God employing to communicate with people in Scripture (listed on Day 6).

6. Expressions of Affection

In an intimate friendship, there are different expressions of affection and extended periodic conversations. The same can be done with God.

Too many marriages have frequent but, ultimately shallow, detail-driven conversations as the only basis for communication. For example, a wife may be crying out for a deep conversation over a candle-lit dinner, but find that day after day her husband's communication is limited to an exchange of information about the schedule, the kids' education, or his own needs. It's the same way with our loving, heavenly Father. He longs to express his love to us and he delights in our expressions of love for him.

7. Honesty

Honesty is extremely important. God wants us to be honest with him, just as we expect honesty from our friends. You will notice in listening prayer times that if there's something bugging you (i.e. a known sin in your life, something you're ticked off at someone about, your own questions about God's wisdom, boredom with your life or your relationship with him), it's really hard to hear God and get truly intimate with him until you've cleared the air regarding whatever issue is bothering you.

Apply It

These seven principles are the key to improving our communication with God. He will allow us to settle for less, but in Jeremiah 29:13 he says, "You will seek me and find me when you seek me with all your heart." A wholehearted seeking involves deep, intimate dialogue laced with expressions of affection. This is one reason God tells us to worship and praise him.

Scripture Meditation

Spend a minute or more just thinking about the following passage: "His sheep follow him because they know his voice." John 10:4

Pray

"How is it that your sheep recognize your voice? What does your voice sound like? Is there anything you'd like to reveal from this passage?" Wait in silence as the Holy Spirit reveals truth to you.

Questions to Ask the Lord

1. Have I picked up any bad habits in the way I communicate with people? What are they?

2. Is there anything you want me to try doing as I attempt to converse with you?

3. Have I failed to expect you to respond or even to give you the time to respond? How so?

4. Are there any questions you'd like me to ask you?

5. Is there anything you'd like to share with me?

DAY EIGHT

HOW TO START A CONVERSATION WITH GOD

I've watched many of my friends' marriages wind up on the rocks. The hardest situations to understand are those where both spouses seem to have good communication skills, but where they have stopped caring for and serving their mate.

Some time ago I counseled a young married couple named Sue and Dave whose marriage was teetering dangerously because Dave had foolishly withheld secrets from his past. When Sue began to uncover those secrets, her world was turned upside down. She didn't know how far she could trust him, or even who this person was that she had married. She felt incredible pain and betrayal. Dave in turn was ashamed and didn't know what to do.

For a long time, it looked as though their marriage would end that first year. Sue wanted to know every detail about how far his betrayal had gone. When Dave was finished sharing the details, she wanted to know more, not knowing if there were further revelations that he was holding back. As Sue kept probing for information where there was nothing left to disclose, Dave wanted to scream, "OK, already—stop torturing me! I'm sorry, I repent!"

After a while, Sue was so sickened by what she had uncovered that she felt as though she was living with a stranger. She couldn't bear the thought of being around him, much less being married to him.

Over time and with much effort, they began to understand one another. They had to start getting to know one another from scratch. They went on dates and were polite to one another. He asked her questions about her interests and her feelings. He learned how to be honest with her. In time, they began to rebuild their relationship, and today, learning about communication saved their marriage. It is finally strong because of commitment and hard work.

Apply It

Sitting down and talking with someone for the first time can be awkward, particularly if that person doesn't communicate in conventional ways.

We see in the New Testament that it was natural to communicate personally with God, but today an entire generation of disciplers is failing to teach this most fundamental of spiritual skills. By studying and applying biblical principles of communication, we can better understand how to converse with our heavenly Father.

Four Steps

We are made in God's image to abide in him and have a personal relationship with him. Jesus himself called us friends. Therefore, conversation with God is like any conversation we have with our friends.

To understand this idea, I recommend the following four steps based on Scripture: 1. Focus 2. Repent 3. Ask 4. Listen

Look up the Scripture passages under each step below.

1. Focus

Begin by meditating on Scripture. God tells us what interests him—he expresses his thoughts and interests in Scriptures like the ones below. He's interested in....

• John 15:9 "As the Father has loved me, so have I loved you." You interest him.
• Zephaniah 3:17 "He will take great delight in you, he will quiet you with his love, he will rejoice over you with singing." You interest him.
• Jeremiah 31:3 "I have loved you with an everlasting love; I have drawn you with loving-kindness." You interest him.
• John 14:1 "Do not let your hearts be troubled." You interest him.
• Matthew 24:14 "And this gospel of the kingdom will be preached in the whole world." Hope for all people.
• 2 Peter 3:9 "...not wanting anyone to perish, but everyone to come to repentance." Salvation for all.
• Matthew 28:19 "Go and make disciples of all nations..." Discipleship for all.
• Isaiah 61:1 "The Lord has anointed me to preach good news to the poor." The poor interest him.
• Isaiah 61:8 "I, the Lord, love justice." Justice interests him.

2. Repent

Ask, "Are we OK?" People don't talk to each other when they've hurt one another. We can grieve the Holy Spirit when he has counseled us and we have spurned his counsel. We may need to repent to reestablish the relationship.

• Jeremiah 13:11 "They have not listened."
• Acts 3:9-19 "You acted in ignorance...repent then... that times of refreshing may come..."
• Revelation 2:5 "Repent and do the things you did at first."

• 1 John 1:9 "If we confess our sins, he is faithful and just and will forgive us our sins and purify us from all unrighteousness."

3. Ask

Ask the Lord. People need something to talk about. We seek the Lord's counsel by asking him questions and listening for his response.

• Isaiah 8:19 "Should not a people inquire of their God?"
• Jeremiah 10:21 "The shepherds are senseless and do not inquire of the Lord."
• Habakkuk 1:2, 2:2 "How long, O Lord...Then the Lord replied."
• 1 Kings 22:5 "Seek the counsel of the Lord."
• Proverbs 8:17 "Those who seek me find me."

4. Listen

Listen for his response. People need to wait for a response to a question. Sometimes it takes a while for our conversational partner to respond. We need to listen, expecting and waiting for an answer.

• 1 Samuel 3:9 "Speak Lord, for your servant is listening."
• Psalm 34:4 "I sought the Lord, and he answered me."
• Proverbs 8:32-33 "Listen to me...listen to my instruction."
• John 10:3, 16, 27 "The sheep listen to his voice." "They too will listen to my voice." "My sheep listen to my voice."

Reading through the above list is only one step in the direction of hearing God in what may be new ways that he wants to speak to you. Once you've come to the place of being able to give intellectual assent to the fact that he has spoken in many ways to people throughout the Bible, and that he may very well do so today, you've begun to let him out of the box that you've had him in.

Now you are positioned to begin looking for the ways that he may be talking to you. God wants you to actually look for and even expect him to carry on his conversation with you through a variety of means.

Scripture Meditation

Spend a minute or more just thinking about the following passage: "Call upon me...and I will listen to you...seek me with all your heart." (Jeremiah 29:12-13)

Pray

"Lord God, I confess that I don't call nearly enough, listen hard enough, and too often, I seek you half-heartedly. What does it mean to seek you with all my heart? What do you want to show me about this Scripture?" Wait in silence as the Holy Spirit reveals truth to you.

Questions to Ask the Lord

Spend some time in prayer.

1. Are there areas of my life where I've kept things from you?

2. What can I do to deepen our relationship?

3. Is there a passage of Scripture that you want to show me?

4. Are there questions that I need to be asking you? What are they?

DAY NINE

GOD SPEAKS THROUGH THE BIBLE

I have personally experienced God's direction through the Scriptures and have heard many accounts of people who sought God's direction in their lives and received it directly from the Bible.

I remember when my grandfather died. I loved him very much and I cherished the time we got to spend together. A big passion of his was playing golf. We spent many mornings together on the public course in Fernandina Beach, Florida. Afterwards we'd talk over a hamburger and coke while he repeatedly told the punch line in jokes, laughing every time.

When Granddad died, I struggled to know that God understood the grief I felt because I hadn't experienced death on this level before. Therefore, it blew me away when God shared with me 2 Corinthians 5:1-4. In this passage, Paul compares our mortal body to a tent. "Now we know that if the earthly tent we live in is destroyed, we have a building from God, an eternal house in heaven...for while we are in this tent, we groan and are burdened..."

Those were exactly the words I needed to hear. They were God's personal words of comfort to his hurting child. His words showed me that he empathized with my grief and held out the hope of life beyond this earth for my grandfather. All of a sudden, my relationship with God was very personal. His words out of Scripture were a great comfort to me. It felt as though he had written them just for me. I knew that he hadn't left me to struggle through this alone – he cared. I felt a wonderful consolation in my loss, and I experienced a revelation of

God's personal love as words on paper leapt off the page and spoke to me.

The Bible is the starting place in our pursuit of a personal relationship with God because it is his revelation of himself to mankind. He revealed himself to us in his inspired, infallible Scriptures because he loves us. It is not only the story of his relationship with people, but also one of the main tools that he uses to communicate with us. God instructs us and guides us using the Bible. Because God uses the Scriptures to speak to us, we look to them for his direction.

Thankfully, in our society we are blessed with the opportunity to own multiple copies of the Bible and to be educated in how to study it.

If you're like me, you began communicating with God relying primarily on the Bible. You learned to respect and venerate it. Since it is unchanging, you can always turn to it—God's words are there in black and white.

The Bible is God's tool for communicating with us. We must understand the value of Scripture. We see in 2 Timothy 3:16-17 that, "all Scripture is God-breathed and is useful for teaching, rebuking, correcting, and training."

Don't Limit God!

Having said this, we need to recognize that anything taken too far can get in the way of the truth. If you never exit your prayer closet into the world, you may lose touch with the world.

Similarly, some of us have substituted a "relationship" with a book for a relationship with God. God can talk to us any way he wants. After all, he's God! He chose many different ways to speak to people in Scripture, and he may choose different ways with us as well. He does not tell us in Scripture that he has limited himself and will only speak to us through the Bible.

As we saw in the Scripture on Day 6 of this devotional, the Bible gives us example after example of a God who speaks not only through Scripture, but also through circumstances—through other people, dreams, impressions, and numerous other means. He used a rooster to convict Peter of his faithlessness. He has probably spoken to you through your friends or family members. He regularly uses pastoral sermons to challenge people to godly living.

He doesn't want us to limit the ways in which we look for him to speak. Some people take the path of least resistance, figuring that God speaks primarily through circumstances. Others rely too heavily on their feelings. Still others are flaky in pursuing every impression that they interpret as coming from God, even when the impressions may contradict Scripture.

God created you. He wants to have a personal relationship with you more than you want to connect with him. Remind yourself, we as Christians often tell nonbelievers, "he loves you!" He didn't just give you a general revelation—he wants you to know him personally as an individual. He knows your worries. He has numbered the hairs on your head and cares for you more than many sparrows. He wants an intimate relationship with you.

The Bible is the account of a God who speaks directly and relationally, not obliquely. Because he is interested in relationship and good communication, we can expect him to be clear.

When we see examples of him speaking using Old Testament Scripture in the New Testament, it is often to confirm what he has said in other ways. As Hebrews 1:1 says, "In the past God spoke to our forefathers through the prophets at many times and in various ways..." There are many examples of this in Acts, the last of which is in Acts 28:25-29, where Paul cites Isaiah to show that God has sent salvation to the Gentiles.

But if you lack experience in hearing God's voice, you can't be blamed for asking whether or not conversation with God is even possible. Restricting yourself to the Bible makes it all so much more clear-cut. You may find yourself asking honest questions like, "Is it supposed to be a kind of monologue, a one-way chattering to the air, or a dialogue?" Or, "If it's meant to be a dialogue, then am I meant to only hear God speak through the Bible like some kind of codebook?"

Apply It

If we truly believe that the Bible is inspired, then we must not try to torture meaning from it to fit our experience. Rather, we should follow the patterns and principles that it gives us.

Scripture Meditation

Spend a minute or more just thinking about the following passage: "All Scripture is God-breathed and is useful for teaching, rebuking, correcting, and training." (2 Timothy 3:16)

Pray

"Heavenly Father, thank you for giving us the gift of Scripture. Thank you for speaking it into existence as you communicated to men and they obediently wrote what they perceived you to say down on parchment. Thank you for the many ways in which it can be used. Is there a particular truth you'd like to show me from this verse?" Wait in silence as the Holy Spirit reveals truth to you.

Questions to Ask the Lord

1. Lord, have I failed to look to the Bible for guidance in my life?

2. Have I failed to keep an open mind about the ways in which you may choose to speak to me? When?

3. How have you chosen to speak to me in the past?

4. What can I do to better trust you in the future?

5. Is there anything you want to say to me?

DAY TEN

GETTING CONTROL OF YOUR THOUGHT LIFE

Several Christmases ago, someone in our family got the computer game called "Myst." That's myst as in "mystery." Perhaps you've seen it or played it. You find yourself on an island that is apparently deserted, with a series of obscure clues that come to light. As you piece together the clues, a story begins to take shape. If you stay at it long enough, you may be able to uncover the mystery.

Our family quickly became absorbed trying to find the clues. We took turns for hours at a time. Each person took notes concerning where they traveled to on the island, as well as what they discovered. It became the main topic of conversation around the house. I would sometimes work at it late into the night.

The kids would ask upon waking up in the morning, "Dad, what did you figure out?"

"Well, I found out that there's a cave."

"What was in the cave?"

"There are a bunch of things you can look at. Some of them are clues and others don't seem to have any significance."

"Did the cave lead you anywhere?"

"No, there is a switch on the wall that might open something, but I couldn't figure it out."

It went for several days. I'm not sure, but I think I began to dream about that dumb game. My mind was wrapped around all the clues.

Eventually we did figure out the mystery, but as I look back on it, I see it was only because of the focused attention we gave to the game. In the process, it took over our thought life. The same dynamic applies to anything we give our attention to for an extended time. Whether it's football on Sunday afternoons or romance novels, our minds tend to follow the familiar territory of past thoughts.

Yesterday we saw that a primary way God speaks to us is through the Bible. As you've meditated on Scripture, perhaps you've seen that. The Lord may have even brought Scriptures to mind that you've memorized in order to communicate with him.

God wants to put the spotlight on your thought life. He wants to exchange your thoughts for his thoughts.

In Philippians 4:8 it says, "Whatever is true, whatever is noble, whatever is right, whatever is pure, whatever is lovely, whatever is admirable – if anything is excellent or praiseworthy – think about such things."

God has deposited his thoughts in Scripture. As we meditate on them, we fill our minds with his thoughts. What better way to get to know someone than to focus on what they've said? Eventually that person's thoughts begin to fill our minds. Sometimes as I meditate on Scripture, I give the Holy Spirit a store of "God thoughts" to bring to my mind later at an appropriate time.

We tend to think about those things that we focus on. One way to crowd out those thoughts that lead us away from God is to exchange them for thoughts based upon Scripture.

Of course, there are other thoughts we can think that will do this as well. Those things that are true, noble, right, pure, lovely, admirable, excellent, and praiseworthy are not necessarily found only in Scripture. They may simply be things we've observed in our workaday world.

Looking further at Philippians 4:9, Paul holds up his own example as one that his Philippian readers should imitate. The example of other godly Christians also illustrates this passage. For example, reading Christian biographies like Rees Howells, Intercessor can set your spiritual sights higher in the same way that meditating on Scripture can (see Recommended Reading at the end of the book).

Apply It

In our society, these kinds of spiritual thoughts too frequently find themselves in competition with a host of other distractions as we immerse ourselves in noise from TV, Game Boys, iPhones, newspapers, radios, DVDs, and unedifying people. No one is suggesting that you become a monk. But it is time to pay attention to your thought life. It is time to regulate what fills your mind.

Scripture Meditation

Spend a minute or more just thinking about the following passage: "Whatever is true, whatever is noble, whatever is right, whatever is pure, whatever is lovely, whatever is admirable—if anything is excellent or praiseworthy— think about such things." (Philippians 4:8)

A good way to apply the Philippians 4 passage is to begin by listing some things that fit under each category that Paul lists. Begin by looking at the list below and start writing things that fit under each category.

After you've done that, spend a minute meditating on each category. Scripture tells us that as we do so, we'll be conformed to Christ's image.

- Whatever is True
- Whatever is Noble
- Whatever is Right
- Whatever is Pure

- Whatever is Lovely
- Whatever is Admirable
- Anything Excellent or Praiseworthy

Pray

"Heavenly Father, please show me how I can begin exchanging my thoughts for yours. Show me which of my thoughts get in the way of your thoughts and what to do about that." Wait in silence as the Holy Spirit reveals truth to you.

Questions to Ask the Lord

1. Pour your heart out to the Lord. Tell him how much you love him, then listen for his response.

2. Lord would you speak to me through your word today? Please lead me to a passage that will speak to me.

DAY ELEVEN

HOW DO WE LISTEN?

Sometimes after a difficult day at the office I'll come home to the usual chaos that five children can create. Here is a typical scene from a few years ago.

I walk into the kitchen by way of the garage door, my mind still caught up in the day's events. Immediately a barrage of information and questions comes from the children.

Leah: "Hi, Daddy... Help me do my shoelaces."

Emily: "Daddy, listen to what happened to me! We went down by the creek to look for salamanders and..."

Seth: "Oh, Dad, you're home. Could you help me with my trigonometry? I haven't been able to figure it out."

Estie: "Dad, am I allowed to see a movie if Talia already saw it? I really want to see it, but mom said that I need to talk to you about it."

Talia: "Yeah, but I got to see it after waiting for years—she needs to wait too."

All the while in the background, others will be talking back and forth. The dog may even be barking. The phone may ring. Meanwhile, I may only be listening with one ear as I go through the mail, looking for and finding an unexpectedly high credit card bill.

I've found that conversation in such a confusing environment can be too difficult, and my listening skills are therefore impaired. If someone says something to me in such a setting, I almost never look at them while they talk. If I reply at all, it'll be a minimal response—probably a grunt.

Over time, I've learned that I need to do a better

job of anticipating and regulating these kinds of sensory overload situations. Now the children know not to ask me questions for the first five minutes that I'm home. When we do interact, I'm more focused and am able to apply some of the listening skills that work when the person I'm talking with has my full attention.

Many people are more interested in what they have to say than listening to another (see Proverbs 18:2). When engaged in conversation, they are lining up their next response while their partner is still speaking. The problem is that not only do they miss what the person's unstated feelings may be, but they also may fail to hear the actual words themselves (see Proverbs 18:13)! Such a person may be prone to interrupt, cutting off their partner in mid-sentence, and speaking right over the top of them.

Listening Skills

We don't come by good conversational skills naturally. If you struggle in listening to people whom you can see, then you are probably going to struggle to listen to God whom you cannot see. We need to learn how to listen – we need to work at it. The following five principles of good listening apply not only to conversations between people, but also to conversations with God.

> 1. Create a space for the other party to speak. Most people need to know that they have your focused attention before they speak. Just as young couples find it difficult to communicate over the sound of screaming children and need to get away from the noise if they are going to connect, so we need uninterrupted time with God. He is not going to compete with wandering thoughts or distractions.

That is why earnest Christians through the ages have emphasized the disciplines of solitude and meditation. Solitude separates us from the demands of our work-a-day world. And meditation involves focusing on one thought for an extended time till it so fills our minds that all our other thoughts are crowded out. Certain places are quieter than others and certain times (such as the early morning hours) are less busy than others.

2. Once alone with your conversation partner, you should look at him or her. When you train your eyes on someone, you pick up nonverbal cues. You become fully alive to their presence. However, with God it is a bit different. An application for our conversations with God could be praising and worshiping him to help us focus our mind's eye on his presence. This is one reason why worship is important. It helps us to better see him. By focusing on him and extending our attention and energy his way, we enter his presence.

3. Ask questions. Questions show interest and they elicit a response from the other party. Most people apprehend only the most superficial things about one another. We go deeper in understanding their desires and thoughts by exchanging information with them. Questions dredge information out into the open air.

4. Acknowledge responses. In a typical conversation, you give feedback. You say "okay," "uh-huh," "I understand," etc., to show that you're following the point. If you're a great listener, experts say, you'll also restate what the other person said. If it's extremely important to you, you'll even take a note. Do the same thing with God. Thank him. Write down your impressions of what he said. Too often God gives us the very thing we're looking for—for example, wisdom

concerning a decision or a particular circumstance—and we fail to adequately acknowledge his grace in our lives.

5. Understand that we are not promised a response. Don't get frustrated by silence. We are promised when we pray according to his will that he hears and grants our request. God may be saying, "Do what you think is best." Replacing Judas was one of the disciples' first important decisions, and they made it by casting lots after waiting on God in prayer! God has given us the Holy Spirit to guide us. You may want to consider whether he may be leaving it up to you to make your best call.

Scripture Meditation

Spend a minute or more just thinking about the following passage: "Be still, and know that I am God; I will be exalted among the nations..." (Psalm 46:10)

Pray

"Lord, why is it important that I am still? How is that related to knowing you? How is that related to your being exalted among the nations?" Wait in silence as the Holy Spirit reveals truth to you.

Questions to Ask the Lord

Spend some time in prayer. Close the door and, either literally or metaphorically, get down on your hands and knees to create an environment of complete focus. Sing or listen to a worship song, or read a psalm or hymn of praise aloud to God.

1. Ask God to free your mind of all other thoughts and concerns for this time of conversation with him. Commit to him that you want to give this time to him and him alone. Ask him to help you focus your mind on him.

2. Is there anything you want to say to me now?

3. Are there any questions you would have me ask you?

Write down any impressions you feel he's giving you. Ask him the questions he gives you.

DAY TWELVE

IMPRESSIONS

*D*uring a recent winter in Philadelphia, a missionary family received the privilege of experiencing the cold and miserable gut of the season. The brick facade of their house was beginning to pull away from its structure and if you looked along the side of the house, you could see it buckling. Eventually a gap appeared. It was extremely dangerous. At one point, a piece of it fell off and almost hit a passerby.

The family's five-year-old daughter had a dream that the whole family moved across the street into another home. They prayed and asked if the Lord was warning them. A coworker thought he heard the Lord saying that the house would be condemned within a month.

However, the missionaries prayed and did not have peace about moving out. A month passed and their home was not condemned. Another month passed and some money was donated to help fix up the facade. Eventually, the old façade was torn down and replaced with a new one.

What do you think? Was the coworker wrong to share what he perceived God to be saying? No, that's not the lesson here. By submitting it for prayer, he gave the missionary family the opportunity to confirm it or not. Therefore, he was not wrong because no one is 100% accurate all the time.

On other occasions, this coworker shared impressions of what the Lord said to him. When tested against Scripture and the passage of time, the words were indeed from God.

Since then, this young man has become more accurate in discerning what God is saying to him. Sometimes he still "misses God" as he humbly submits an impression of what God may have said for review by a fellow Christian. Doing this can seem risky, but he sharpens his hearing and proves himself trustworthy to the Lord.

Some people who are prone to seeing the world in black and white terms may struggle with this. "Would God ever be so imprecise? Why would he allow us to misinterpret him like that?" Yet look at such a person's life, and you'll find that they have missed God as frequently as anybody else! That's the human condition—we're all fallible.

1 Corinthians 13:12 says, "Now we see but a poor reflection as in a mirror... Now I know in part; then I shall know fully, even as I am fully known."

The Pharisees had a narrowly defined view of how God could speak. Instead of helping them draw near to him, this view only set them up as antagonists of Jesus. Those who said, "God only speaks through the Bible," still have to identify particular passages, interpret them, and apply them. Good, godly people constantly disagree over which passages to use, how they should be interpreted, and then how they should be applied.

Where Thoughts Come From

All thoughts are not our own. Just as the devil can insert a tempting thought into our brains, so can the Holy Spirit insert a thought. If this weren't true, we wouldn't have been told to take every thought captive (2 Corinthians 10:4-5). If this weren't true, what role would the Holy Spirit have in leading us to repentance? Where does that spontaneous desire to show love for another come from, if not from God?

As Romans 3:12 says, "There is no one who does good, not even one." If we agree that the Holy Spirit gives us thoughts or counsel periodically, how do we distinguish these thoughts from other thoughts? Some people call these thoughts, "impressions from the Lord." Impressions are thoughts that flit and flash on the screen of our minds. Our minds receive hundreds of impressions a day. Some impressions may be temptations whispered by the enemy, while others may be the Holy Spirit speaking to us.

We sometimes conclude that Paul and the other apostles never had to struggle with wondering whether a desire or a hunch they had was actually from God. But we see them in frequent conflict in the book of Acts. In Acts 15:36, Paul and Barnabas wanted to make a return visit to their mission churches. Where did this desire come from? Perhaps God was speaking to Paul through his natural inner motivation to see people grow. Or, perhaps Paul heard the Lord whisper to him. In either case, they immediately disagreed about how to do it and parted company.

Impressions often seem very much like our own thoughts. The Holy Spirit may speak to us in an impression—a voice so still and small that it is easy to dismiss as being our own thought. Indeed, most American Christians probably do dismiss this voice, and so never sharpen their spiritual hearing.

If we were able to immediately recognize his voice, the Christian walk would only be a matter of obedience. Discernment and wisdom would not play such an important role in our lives. However, the fact is that we refine our senses by focusing on them. That is how a blind person refines the senses of touch and hearing far beyond the level of those of us who see. He focuses on them.

Growing In Discernment

In the same way we refine our ability to discern God's voice. Because we are so unfamiliar with it, we struggle to recognize it at first. We may experience more failure than success. Yet we must struggle to grow and shrink from failure if we are to mature in our faith.

As we listen for God, we recognize that some other foolish thing is likely to pop into our minds instead. We acknowledge that it may seem impossible to distinguish the fleshly thoughts from God-initiated ones. We try to deal with this problem by sharing with others the impressions we receive, judging them against what God does subsequently and in view of the Scriptures.

In some cases, there may be no correlation between what you thought God was saying and what actually happens. However, in other cases, the specificity of what you have been shown in prayer lines up so well with what God does, there can be no doubt that God has spoken to you. When you see that God actually did speak, not only does your faith in him grow, but your faith in your own ability to hear grows as well.

Because we can be so fallible in our hearing—one moment interpreting our stray thoughts as directives and the next writing off the Holy Spirit's promptings—we need to start paying attention to our thought life. To grow in this skill of distinguishing between your impressions of God's voice and your own thoughts, you have to take some risks. It's like riding a bicycle. You have to be willing to take a few falls in order to master it. You have to be willing to say, "These may just be my own thoughts and not God speaking, but this is the impression I received."

Apply It

To test whether an impression is from God or not, test it against the points listed in Day Two of this devotional. If it's a toss-up, pray about it with some others, and then do what you think God is asking you to do, even though you're unsure. This is how you grow in your discernment. God will honor your earnest desire and as you debrief with your accountability partner, he'll show you how to better distinguish his voice next time. We learn by taking risks—no risks, no increasing of your trust. No trust, no "getting on the bicycle." No getting on the bicycle, no progress.

Scripture Meditation

Spend a minute or more just thinking about the following passage: "My thoughts are not your thoughts." (Isaiah 55:8)

Pray

"Heavenly Father, have I mistaken my thoughts for your thoughts? Do I know your thoughts? How can I better distinguish between your thoughts and mine? What do you want me to get out of this passage?" Wait in silence as the Holy Spirit reveals truth to you.

Questions to Ask the Lord

1. Sometimes I struggle to distinguish between my own thoughts and your voice. How can I tell the difference between the two?

2. Was there ever an impression that you gave me that I dismissed because I thought it was merely

one of my own thoughts, but was actually from you?

3. Have I ever given you credit for an impression when it was just my own thoughts? What was that?

4. What do you want me to do to hear your voice better?

5. Is there anything you want to share with me today?

DAY THIRTEEN

OTHER WAYS GOD SPEAKS

*K*aren and I lived in West Palm Beach, Florida for seven years. Towards the end of the seventh year, we began to sense that God wanted us to move somewhere else that we didn't know.

We looked at Colorado Springs, Dallas, and Atlanta. We felt that he wanted us to be within an hour's drive of a major international airport in an inexpensive, family-friendly environment.

Eventually we settled on one of three towns an hour's drive from Atlanta. Then God confirmed through a variety of circumstances, Scriptures, and other means, that Gainesville, Georgia was to be our new location.

We put our Florida house on the market and took a couple of house-hunting trips to Gainesville. We were tired of life in the suburbs and began looking for a piece of property in the country where we could build our own home.

Within a month, the Florida home sold and we began to feel desperate. What if we couldn't find a place? We'd scoured all of north Georgia and couldn't find anything within our price range. In another few weeks, we'd be forced to move all our stuff and we didn't have any place to go to!

One night Karen and I were discussing our situation as we prepared for bed. She said, "I just read a book by Dick Eastman where they were in a situation like ours and he anointed a For Sale sign with oil and God answered his prayer. I'm going to do that, and what's more, I think that we should pray for a dream." We had never prayed for a dream before; I was skeptical.

"That's great, dear. I'll pray that God gives you a dream tonight."

"No, you're the head of the house, I'm going to pray that you get the dream!" she exclaimed, and proceeded to pray right then before we drifted off to sleep.

Early the next morning, I had the dream she'd prayed for! I woke up amazed that God had answered the prayer. In the dream I saw our two-story house on land we were going to buy from a man named Tom.

The next week, I happened to be in the Gainesville area at a conference. On a whim before leaving town, I looked in the classified ads. There was a piece of property that seemed perfect, and when I saw it, I knew it was the very property God had set aside for us.

The next week, we moved all of our stuff out of the Florida home and drove up to Gainesville. I went and negotiated a deal with the owner the next day and yes, his name was Tom!

God's Whispers

It's rare in my experience that God speaks in such dramatic ways. If you look at the hundreds of decisions made in a week, (even if you pray continually as the Bible suggests) it is far more common for the Father to speak to you in a quiet voice requiring faith to believe and follow through in obedience.

Because this book is about helping you learn how you can talk conversationally with your heavenly Father, I've emphasized the often subtle way that the Holy Spirit communicates by whispering to our spirit. At the same time, as noted in Day 6, he is not limited in the means that he uses.

You'll recall we listed a variety of methods: through Scripture, others, circumstances, audibly, inwardly, through dreams, visions, and demonstrations of power. Because some of these methods may seem rather dramatic, they don't so much evoke a conversational response in us as they evoke a sense of awe and worship.

An impression is more commonplace and more difficult to discern than when God speaks inwardly. When God speaks inwardly, his voice sounds as clear to you as if it were coming from someone in the same room. It is as though he did speak audibly. Though not heard by others, his spoken inward voice is unmistakable. It crashes through your consciousness with a timbre and authority that stops you in your tracks.

In Isaiah 55:8 God says, "My thoughts are not your thoughts." When you hear his thoughts expressed in words, they "sound" different than your own thoughts and are clear. Many Christians occasionally "hear" God speak to them inwardly. We need to distinguish this communication from the everyday impressions we receive that may or may not be the Holy Spirit nudging us in a particular direction.

Earlier we studied some of the different ways in which God speaks. Let's look at some new Scriptures and again study ways that God has chosen to speak to people.

Through Scripture

• Acts 8:32-33 "The eunuch was reading... Scripture..." he was reading a messianic prophecy from Isaiah 53, setting him up to ask Philip about the Messiah.
• Luke 4:17-21 "Today this Scripture is fulfilled...." Jesus quotes Isaiah 61.

SETH BARNES

Through Others

• Acts 1:8 "You will be my witnesses." Jesus describes the way in which he will speak to the nations: through them!
• Acts 8:34-35 "Philip...told him the good news about Jesus." God guided Philip to the head of finance for the Ethiopian kingdom to lead him to Christ.

Circumstances/Events

• Acts 17:5-10 Paul and Silas leave Thessalonica because of persecution. They flee to Berea when it is no longer safe.

Impressions

• Ephesians 3:16-19 Knowing Christ's love. The width, length, height, and depth of Christ's love are grasped in a way that surpasses knowledge.
• Colossians 1:9 Spiritual wisdom. We are filled with the knowledge of his will through spiritual wisdom and understanding.

Audibly

• Matthew 3:17 "A voice from heaven..." Jesus gets God's blessing on the occasion of his baptism.
• Acts 9:4-7 "He fell to the ground and heard a voice." Jesus confronts Paul with a question that changes his life.
• Acts 8:26-29 "An angel of the Lord said to Philip..." An angel, one of God's messengers, gives Philip directions to Gaza.

Inwardly

• 1 Chronicles 14:14-16 "David inquired of God... God answered." David had the habit of asking God for his opinion every time he got into a scrape, which was often.
• Ezekiel 12:1 "The word of the Lord came to me." Ezekiel hears a very specific message from God, not as a vision or a dream, but as words demanding action.

Through Surprising Means

• Job 38:1 A storm. The Lord chooses an awe-inspiring vehicle for his message to Job.
• Numbers 22:30 A donkey. God uses an animal to convict Balaam of his sin.

Through Visions

• Daniel 4:5 "The visions that passed through my mind terrified me." Nebuchadnezzar's visions felt so real and were so harrowing that he was scared to death.
• Acts 10:10-19 Peter "fell into a trance." The key issue–the particulars of the new covenant– is communicated to Peter in a way he is sure to remember.
• Acts 16:9 "Paul had a vision." The Lord gives Paul a vision to communicate a course correction.

Through Dreams

• Genesis 40:8 "Do not interpretations belong to God? Tell me your dreams." Joseph, having had a few dreams of his own, knows that God uses them

to communicate, even to kings.
• Joel 2:28 "I will pour out my Spirit on all people...
your old men will dream dreams." God promises
to repay his people for the years the locusts have
eaten.

Through Demonstrations of Power

• 1 Corinthians 4:20 "The kingdom of God is not
a matter of talk but of power." Paul challenges his
antagonists to a duel based on God's power.
• 1 Thessalonians 1:5 The "gospel came to you
not simply with words, but also with power." The
Thessalonians believed so quickly because God
backed up Paul's words with miracles.

Scripture Meditation

Spend a minute or more just thinking about the following
passage: "I will pour out my Spirit on all people. Your
sons and daughters will prophesy, your old men will
dream dreams, your young men will see visions." (Joel
2:28)

Do you remember the time before email existed?
People called more and used "snail mail" more. Would
you want to suddenly be the only one not to be able to
be reached by email? In the same way God wants you to
be open to him speaking to you in new ways. If you are
afraid of allowing God to speak to you in a new way, then
share your feelings with him.

Pray

"Lord, if you want to speak to me in a variety of ways,
please prepare me. If you want to speak to me in a new

way, you need to make it very clear to me that it is you."
Wait in silence as the Holy Spirit reveals truth to you.

Questions to Ask the Lord

Spend some time in prayer.

> 1. As I'm reading the Bible today, please give me a
> special verse that will speak to me in an area of my
> life in which I need to hear from you.
>
> 2. Ask the Lord to give you other questions to ask
> him today...
>
> 3.
>
> 4.
>
> 5.

Think about the ocean or go sit on the beach, if you
can. If you can't go, close your eyes and really imagine
being there. Watch the water, listen to the waves, smell
the salt, feel the sand. God says that his love for you is
deeper than the ocean. Take time to really ponder that.
If it is hard for you to accept, ask God to break down any
walls in your heart that are keeping out his love.

DAY FOURTEEN

CAN GOD TRUST YOU?

*E*arlier, I shared a story about our daughter's dog, Whimsy. Whimsy has just one problem: he doesn't know his limitations. We live on a farm, so if you're a dog, the potential for mischief is great.

A little fluff ball of a dog has no business out among the stray dogs, deer, and coyotes that prowl the edges of our property. On the odd occasion when Whimsy gets loose, he inevitably heads for the adventurous woods behind our house. Consequently, we have a rule that he must be walked on a leash. However, some days in winter when it is so dark and cold, it's easier to let Whimsy out on his own than to escort him around.

One gray winter day, we opted for convenience and let him out the front door. When we next looked outside, he was gone. Clad in pajamas and bathrobes, we broke into two search parties and went in opposite directions.

Out to the neighbor's house-nothing. Out to the front of the property—nothing. In the woods behind the house—nothing. The minutes ticked by. We couldn't help but think of our scruffy little bundle of canine energy being devoured by wild animals.

Finally, deep in the woods, we heard the distant yipping of a small dog. After walking long minutes in the direction of the noise, there was Whimsy. He had gone exploring and was on the other side of the barbed wire fence, stuck in a bramble patch. His long black hair had wrapped itself around the thorny stickers.

It took a pair of scissors to cut Whimsy loose. Hanging his head, he was obviously ashamed of the circumstances in which he found himself. Back home, he quickly darted into his kennel for a much-deserved "time out."

We humans are so much like Whimsy! God speaks to us and we disregard what he says, proving that we can't be trusted. We spend time seeking the Lord, we hear from him, and then we fail to follow through on what he's shared with us.

The Bible says, "Foolishness is bound up in the heart of a child." (Proverbs 22:15) God gives us many blessings in life and he provides us with clear boundaries.

In his house we are fed and cared for. But we are enticed by the adventure of the deep woods. Something inside us yearns to go beyond the boundaries we've established. Given our independence, we explore, unaware of the dangers we face.

Then one day when we are caught in the snare of our circumstances, our reality comes crashing down around us. We recognize our peril and the foolishness that got us there, and we cry out for mercy. Time and again our heavenly Father reaches down and spares us from the consequences of our poor choices.

However, sometimes we find ourselves seemingly beyond the reach of his mercy, trapped in a situation we didn't comprehend. We whine, but our choices bring us pain. (Proverbs 5:22)

The lesson to be learned is that of becoming trustworthy to God. He knows the dangers that imperil us. He is our protector. He has given us boundaries for own good, not to fence us in. A trip to the deep woods may seem like adventure for the moment, but ultimately we are trapped by the consequences of our actions and must throw ourselves at the mercy of our heavenly Father.

Can God trust you? He told you to pick up your

cross and follow him. Have you laid down your cross and followed your own way? Do you find yourself caught in the briars? The Lord will chase you down and allow you to feel the consequences of your actions—not because he is mean-spirited, but because he wants to help you avoid getting stuck again! When he calls, he wants to know that you will come. Just as we want to know that we can trust God, so he wants to be able to trust us as well.

Scripture Meditation

Spend a minute or more just thinking about the following passage: "They did what your power and will had decided beforehand should happen." (Acts 4:28)

Pray

"With Paul I can say, 'I have the desire to do what is good, but I cannot carry it out.' I struggle with my flesh. I want to become trustworthy. When you share something with me, I want to be able to carry it with me and be faithful to you. Show me myself, Lord. Where do I struggle most? Show me how to become someone you can trust." Wait in silence as the Holy Spirit reveals truth to you.

Questions to Ask the Lord

Spend some time in prayer. Tell God about how you feel today. Are you in the middle of difficult circumstances? Tell God, pour out your heart to him. Write down what you feel he is saying.

Meditate on Zephaniah 3:17. "The Lord your God is with you, he is mighty to save. He will take great delight in you, he will quiet you with his love, he will rejoice over you with singing."

Sing some praise and worship songs quietly before the Lord. Then ask God: "Lord, what do you sing over me?"

DAY FIFTEEN

FOLLOWING THROUGH

*P*aul Miller was a bear of a man who ministered in the prisons of north Georgia with his wife in the 80s and early 90s. They had a team of people who ministered with them that Miller constantly challenged to get out of their comfort zones.

Miller's trademark was a guitar he carried around like a Mexican bandolero. Because he was so big, the guitar seemed small in comparison. He was always getting the inmates to sing along to the music. As the ministry was doing well, many inmates gave their hearts to Jesus as a result of the testimonies and love shared.

One of the team members received a very disturbing message from the Lord one day. He got a clear impression that God was going to take Miller and his wife home and that they were going to die. In fact, he felt the Lord saying that they were going to die within two months.

At first, he didn't want to share this with anyone. The thought that it might actually happen was horrifying. But the impression was so strong that finally he got the courage to share it—first with the leaders and then with the rest of the team.

When they were gathered, he said, "I know this is a terrible thing to share, but I believe God said, 'Prepare for this ministry to be transferred within the next two months.'" He then shared the specifics of what he felt God had shown him.

You can imagine the impact this had on the rest of the team. A number of the team members rebuked the man who had gotten this impression. But Miller

SETH BARNES

silenced them. After praying about it, Miller sensed that this might in fact be what God was saying, and he had a peace about it. As hard as it was, he began to get his affairs in order and appointed a successor (the man who later shared with me the details of this story) should anything happen.

At the end of two months, Miller and his wife were in a bad car accident in which they were critically injured. They were pulled out of their wrecked car and loaded into an ambulance that sped toward the hospital. As they drove, Miller lifted his head and weakly asked the paramedic, "How's my wife?"

"She's gone," came the reply. On hearing this, Miller nodded, and breathed his last.

When the news reached the team, they reacted with a mixture of grief and awe because God had tenderly prepared them for the loss of their leader.

Once You've Heard

When God has given you a directive, first write it down so that you don't forget it. Test it according to the scriptural pattern given in the Day Two devotional. Then, obey him. God doesn't speak just to sound off. When he shares something with us, he wants us to act on it!

Apply It

Too many people are interested only in the relational dimension of their conversation with God. Our heavenly Father wants us not only to commune with him, but he wants us to persevere. Look up the following passages to better understand what the Bible says about the matter.

• Ezekiel 11:20 "They will follow my decrees."

- Proverbs 8:32 "Blessed are those who keep my ways."
- Acts 5:29 "We must obey God rather than men!"
- John 14:23 "If anyone loves me, he will obey my teaching."
- Hebrews 4:7b "Today, if you hear his voice, do not harden your hearts."

Evaluating What Happened

Just as we often misunderstand one another, so it is that we can misunderstand God. Perhaps he said something and we didn't hear him correctly, or we misinterpreted what he said, or we misapplied it. That's okay—God can handle it!

As babies we didn't learn to communicate with our parents overnight. It took decades for us to be able to communicate with our parents. Many of us still haven't learned!

When I was two years old, my parents would point into the night sky at the moon and tell me about it. Before long, when I'd catch sight of the moon, I'd point at it and excitedly exclaim, "Ee da moon?"

Now many years later, my father and I might carry on a conversation about the impact of the lunar gravitational pull upon tides, and the new technologies facilitating tidal power generation and how, in essence, we are capturing energy from the moon. But our initial conversation began with, "Ee da moon?"

Look at what a complex task it is to learn to communicate with our parents: First, we learn to recognize their voices, then we learn their vocabulary, how to decipher their meaning, how to speak words, how to interact, then lastly, we learn how to respect and obey.

Ultimately, not until our 20s and 30s will we learn

to communicate with our parents on a mature level. It's the same way with God.

Our understanding of how to communicate develops over a long period of time. That's why it's so important to assess our interactions with him after the fact so that we can better understand what worked (and what didn't).

This practice—today we call it "debriefing"—is found throughout Scripture:

> • Luke 2:19 "Mary treasured up all these things and pondered them in her heart."
> • Luke 24:14-15 "They were talking with each other about everything that had happened."
> • 1 Corinthians 14:29 "The others should weigh carefully what is said."
> • Luke 10 The debriefing with Jesus after the 72 had gone out.

Scripture Meditation

Spend a minute or more just thinking about the following passage: "We must obey God rather than men!" (Acts 5:29).

Pray

"Lord, I want my first impulse to be to follow you no matter the cost. I confess that I often lose courage or conviction, or just plain forget, or even willfully disobey. What do you have to show me about obedience?" Wait in silence as the Holy Spirit reveals truth to you.

Questions to Ask the Lord

Spend some time in prayer. Ask the Lord the questions below. Wait for him to respond and write down your impression of what he may be saying.

1. Do I struggle in the area of obedience?

2. Is there anything within me that needs to die so that I can better obey you?

3. What have you shared with me that I've failed to do?

4. Do I pause sufficiently to evaluate my interactions with you?

5. What do you want me to do today?

DAY SIXTEEN

LISTENING LEADS TO MINISTRY

*O*ne of the great joys of my life is to see my children encounter God for themselves. It thrills me to see them personally discover what I know to be true about our Lord. I've found that the best way to impart this is by allowing them to have experiences for themselves.

In the spring of 2001, I accompanied two of my daughters as they went through a ministry seminar and outreach in downtown Atlanta, Georgia. Before going out to minister, we prayed for God's direction, paused to listen, then gathered together as a group to debrief what we perceived he said.

For some members, this probably seemed audacious. It was a threat to the notion that God doesn't really guide his children that often. However, as we debriefed, participants shared what God had brought to mind.

The Lord directed one of the outreach participants, Joan, to give a white cloth cross she had in her Bible to someone. God directed us with this message to go along with the cross: "This is how God sees you: you're pure, clean, and white."

Later, Joan met a man who was in the last stages of AIDS with a month left to live. His face was disfigured with open sores and pneumonia had set in.

The Lord spoke to Joan, "This is the one to receive the cross." Joan was blown away. Here she looked at this man and saw his disfigured face. But this isn't how Jesus saw the man. When Jesus looked at him, he saw him without spot or blemish, clean and white—just like Joan's cloth cross.

Another outreach participant prayed and saw a vision of a trailer house, half of which was painted blue. Later, as our group walked down the street, they spotted the very same half-blue trailer. With their faith boosted, the group went over to it and knocked on the door.

As a man came to the door and looked out through the screen, a group member said, "We're out praying for people in the neighborhood and felt God guiding us to you. Is there anything we can pray for you about?"

At this point, the man opened the screen door and began to share his story. His wife had recently died. "How did you know I needed prayer?" he asked. Of course, Jesus knew the man's need and sent our group as his ambassadors.

Our group became Jesus' hands and feet to this man. They ministered to him and cried together, mourning the loss of his wife. He experienced Jesus' love because group members were willing to take a risk and trust that God might be directing them in a way that they couldn't have anticipated.

As my children participated in this experiment in following the Lord's guidance, they grew far more than if I would have tried to teach them in a classroom.

Learning to Minister

According to Jesus, our purpose in life is to love God and love others. (Mark 12:30-31) The Bible teaches that we are ministers of reconciliation—reconciling man to God, serving as Christ's ambassadors.

In 2 Corinthians 5:18, 20, it says, "God... gave us the ministry of reconciliation... We are therefore Christ's ambassadors, as though God were making his appeal through us." An ambassador is one who acts on behalf of another. We act on God's behalf first by understanding his agenda and mission, then by seeking further direction concerning the specifics of a particular task or initiative.

Many Christians do not understand their roles as God's ambassadors, what his agenda is, or how to seek him for further direction. Consequently, they may miss out on the best Spirit-directed ministry opportunities.

In the absence of a clear picture of God's agenda, most Christians fall back into the default mode of "good works." Skilled ambassadors regularly communicate with headquarters to better understand what they should do. They may or may not receive any further instructions. If they don't, they continue in line with their last communications. If they do, they move forward with those new orders confidently, knowing that their agenda is clear and backed by the full authority of those who sent them.

So how do we move from a passive posture to the position of an ambassador who understands the Lord's intentions, and is prepared to represent Jesus in order to capture hearts for the Lord?

People need to experiment a bit before they are able to change their behavior. It takes a while to try out new things and see if they fit or not. That's why participating in a local ministry or a mission trip is a great place to learn how to begin operating in this new role as God's representative, his ambassador in the world. When we focus on ministry for an extended time, we set aside our own agendas so that we can pursue his agenda – the Great Commission!

When we participate in local ministry or go on a mission trip, it makes sense that the first step in acting as his ambassador is to seek the Lord in order to understand his overarching agenda and what he would have us do on any given day.

This process of asking the Lord for his agenda involves asking the Lord a question and listening for his response. By connecting the practice of listening prayer with local ministry or a mission trip, you give God the opportunity to introduce a corrective if you're off base or missing an even better opportunity.

Your prayer is, "Lord, show me how and where and to whom you want me to minister." You give God the opportunity to respond. You debrief this response. You move out in obedience. Then you evaluate the whole interaction. In doing so, you recognize where you actually did hear him correctly.

The acronym I use to describe this process is ALOE: Ask, Listen, Obey, Evaluate.

A Word of Caution

If listening prayer is not guided or connected with a specific action and debriefed, it can degenerate into flakiness, wherein every stray thought is seen as God's prompting.

Scripture Meditation

Spend a minute or more just thinking about the following passage: "I am sending you out like sheep among wolves." (Matthew 10:16)

Pray

"Jesus, I thank you that your method has always been to send your disciples out and I confess that too often, I get in a comfort zone. You have called me a sheep and called yourself a shepherd. You tell us there are enemies. Please show me what this means for me today. I pray that your truth would find its way to my heart today." Wait in silence as the Holy Spirit reveals truth to you.

Questions to Ask the Lord

1. Is there a practical way that I can practice what I'm learning in ministry?

2. Is there a particular person or place where you want me to minister today?

3. Are you asking me to reach out to others through some kind of ministry?

4. Where and when should I go?

5. Is there anyone who can help me grow in this area of ministering? Who?

DAY SEVENTEEN

THE ROLE OF THE HOLY SPIRIT

I have a friend who once had a client who lived in an unfinished home. It was a finished walk-out basement which never had been built upon. When it was first built, the plans called for a house that had the basement as one of its features. However, for some reason, they never completed the rest of the house. What an odd, unnatural situation. The flooring for the first floor had become the roof!

Did these people have a home? Yes. Was this home all that it could be? No. This family could have lived in much greater freedom, space, and light yet they were content to live in the foundation itself. This is how a lot of believers are because they live in the *logos* foundation of scripture alone, content to live off of the record of God's revelation to others and their intimate relationships with him.

There are two Greek words for "word" in Scripture. The written word is *logos* and the living word is *rhema*. While we are not to depart from the truths of that revelation, God continues to reveal how we apply these truths to our particular lives now and how to direct us into the future.

As a practical matter, we must come to grips with our understanding of the Holy Spirit as our helper and teacher. Jesus said, "It is for your good that I am going away. Unless I go away, the counselor will not come to you." (John 16:7)

Do we really believe that? Do we have a practical confidence in the power of the Holy Spirit as Christ's presence? Do we see manifestations of that power regularly in our ministry?

A famous evangelist has been credited with saying, "I suspect that if the Holy Spirit were removed from the earth, 90% of ministry would continue just as though nothing had ever happened." Would this be true of our ministry? If this is true, then the first place we must begin to remedy the situation is with clear communication between God and us. Power cannot be deployed unless God's specific purposes in a given situation are clear, so that faith and obedience can be exercised.

The Holy Spirit applies God's written word and gives us decision-making wisdom—in other words, good counsel. That's why Jesus refers to him as our counselor. If I don't ask for his counsel and I study God's written word as a history book instead of applying it to my life, then I miss his interaction with me. As previously mentioned, this living word, or instructions for how to live my life, has a different Greek source word, *rhema*.

Those of us who have been raised in the church understand the doctrine of the Trinity. But if someone who knew nothing about that doctrine were to go into some of our churches, he or she might come away thinking that the Trinity is the Father, the Son, and the Bible. Many of us are taught much more about the Bible than we are the person of the Holy Spirit.

Think about it—imagine yourself as a child whose parents have to leave on a long trip. But before going, they introduce you to a new governess who will stay with you at all times. This person, they tell you, will serve as your teacher, counselor, and comforter. Wouldn't you want to get to know her? How much more then, should we be eager to know the third person of the Trinity?

Scripture

Choose and look up some of the following Scriptures, and write what you learn about the roles and responsibilities of the Holy Spirit.

- John 14:16: The Father will give us a
- John 14:17: He is called the Spirit of
- John 14:17: The world does not
- John 14:17: He will be in
- John 16:8-11: He will convict in regard to
- John 16:13: He will guide us into
- John 16:13: He will tell you
- John 16:14: He will bring glory to
- 1 John 2:27: His anointing teaches us about
- Romans 8:26: He helps us when we are
- Romans 8:26: He intercedes with us with
- Romans 8:27: He searches our
- Ephesians 1:17: He is the Spirit of
- Ephesians 1:17: He helps us know
- 1 Corinthians 2:10: He searches
- 1 Corinthians 2:11: He knows
- 1 Corinthians 2:12: He helps us understand
- 1 Corinthians 2:13: He teaches us

Scripture Meditation

Spend a minute or more just thinking about the following passage: "It is for your good that I am going away. Unless I go away, the counselor will not come to you." (John 16:7)

Pray

"Holy Spirit, you are my helper, counselor, and comforter. Jesus said that it was actually a good thing that he would go away so that you would come. Why is that so?" Wait in silence as the Holy Spirit reveals truth to you.

Questions to Ask the Lord

Spend some time in prayer. Ask the Lord the questions below. Wait for him to respond.

1. Do I seek your Spirit's counsel before I make decisions, or do I make them on my own?

2. How do I control my own life and shut you out?

3. What areas do you want me to yield control to you?

4. Am I failing to trust you in any way?

5. How, specifically, can I grow in this area?

DAY EIGHTEEN

LEARNING TO PRAY CONTINUALLY

*H*ere are a couple more of my own journal entries:

8/21/02
Lord, is there anything I've done to hurt our relationship?

Have no other gods before me. No idols. Whatever consumes your thoughts takes my place.

If I may be so bold, I need for you to speak more clearly. I'm slowed by my skepticism and hindered by my rational mind. Help me to love as Jesus loved. Help me to disciple others.

• 1 Corinthians 7:29: "The time is short." Don't be engrossed by the things of the world.
• 1 Corinthians 7:35: "Live in a right way in undivided devotion to the Lord."

8/24/02
Show me where I've fallen short or quenched your Spirit lately.

It's a question of focus. Where do you spend your time? It shows how important I am to you. To build our relationship, spend time with me. Make me your first priority. "Anyone who loves his son or daughter more than me is not worthy of me." (Matthew 10:37)

The irony is, more than a year has passed since I wrote those journal entries and I continue to struggle with these issues. Just because God has spoken to me doesn't mean that I've been successful in applying what he said. He instructed me about focus, yet a year later, I still struggle with focus.

A conversation with God may start in your journal. But a journal, while helpful, is only a tool and as such can begin to feel artificial, or a poor substitute for real, verbal give-and-take.

What starts out as a helpful aid to communication can become rote. For that reason, it's important that you make an effort to move beyond the comfort zone of your devotional time and this devotional and make sure you experience life—even as you walk about the streets and shops in your own community.

Too often, we stereotype prayer. It's that time when we close our eyes, begin with, "Dear God" and close with, "Amen." The Bible says that we should "pray continually." (1 Thessalonians 5:17) We do that as we converse with our Lord throughout the day, telling him our thoughts and struggles, asking him questions and awaiting his responses. Our lives can be a continual process of talking with and listening to God.

Although some people seem to hear the Lord's voice fairly clearly, everyone struggles initially. God's voice has a certain resonance, a pitch and tone that we come to recognize as much as we recognize anyone's voice – through experience and over time. We have to practice tuning in until it begins to come naturally.

As we go through our day, there are things that God wants to remind us about, or even direction he wants to give. Isaiah 30:21 says, "Whether you turn to the right or to the left, your ears will hear a voice behind you, saying, 'This is the way; walk in it.'" When we hear his voice we must go where he leads.

Scripture Meditation

Spend a minute or more just thinking about the following passage: "Be joyful always; pray continually; give thanks in all circumstances…" (1 Thessalonians 5:16-18)

Pray

"Lord, how in the world do you expect me to pray continually? I have a hard time imagining what that might look like. Where do I even start? Give me something today that will help me understand how to get my mind around this thing you've told me to do. I want to be in conversation with you, but I confess that it often feels like a task, rather than something that just flows from me. Show me what a breakthrough would look like. Wait in silence as the Holy Spirit reveals truth to you.

Questions to Ask the Lord

Spend some time in prayer. Ask the Lord some questions:

1. Is my life in balance? What needs to change?

2. Is there anything in my schedule that shouldn't be?

3. With the things that must be done, how can I live in undivided devotion to you?

4. Ask the Lord to give you the questions to ask him…

DAY NINETEEN

DEALING WITH DISTRACTION

*O*ne morning, recognizing that my children are growing up and leaving the nest, I wrote them a letter:

Dear children,

Some of you have already graduated out of our home into the big, bad world. I'll miss the times we had together in the morning. The Lord used our commitment to one another to focus us, to help us seek first his kingdom and his righteousness.

As you make your way in the world, you'll find that you're bombarded by distractions from a number of angles. Your good intentions will get watered down by your commitments. I'm 45 and I haven't figured it all out. I still find my priorities getting out of whack. So, I wanted to share with you a few things I've found to be true that may help you. As Paul said to Timothy, "Finish the race and keep the faith." (2 Timothy 4:7)

To know Jesus, we must learn to listen to his voice. Then to listen, we must focus. Sit in a crowded room where multiple conversations are within earshot and you can actually tune into first one conversation and then another, as you apply your powers of focusing.

It's a remarkable ability God has given us. We can switch our attention from one thing to another like we switch TV channels.

God doesn't want to compete for our attention. He'll wait for our pinball brains to stop bouncing from one thing to the next and settle in on him. Luke 8:14 highlights worries, riches and pleasures as being big obstacles to our ability to focus.

Hey kiddos, remember I'm not intending to preach here. I've just stumbled a few times along life's road. I've found that God wants to help pick me up and his presence in my life is the one thing I most want to pass along to you all.

Love,
Dad

Things That Distract Us

When Jesus lists the three things that are most likely to rob us of his communication, we see that the first two (pleasures and worries) are competitors for our attention.

2 Timothy 2:4 says, "No one serving as a soldier gets involved in civilian affairs." In other words, God isn't going to wrestle for "mindshare"—we have to pray about what pleasures or worries may be distracting us from him.

The devil knows that he has multiple opportunities to interrupt God's work from the time that we receive the word of God to the time that we allow it to guide our behavior. A cynical heart or distracted mind can prevent the word from ever taking root. When the word of God doesn't take root, convicting us to change our behavior, the passage of time may be all that is necessary to weaken our will. When the time to obey comes and we're faced with the opportunity to obey or not obey, it is easy to stop short of obedience.

James 1:22, says, "Do not merely listen to the word, and so deceive yourselves. Do what it says." James goes on to declare that a follower of Jesus should look intently (focus) on what God has said, "not forgetting what he has heard, but doing it – he will be blessed in what he does." (v.25)

Scripture Meditation

Spend a minute or more just thinking about the following passage: "The seed on good soil stands for those with a noble and good heart, who hear the word, retain it, and by persevering produce a crop...Therefore consider carefully how you listen." (Luke 8:15, 18)

Pray

"Lord, I want good soil! I want to retain the word you give me, so that it can grow and bear fruit in my life. Show me what distractions are preventing that. Lord, what do you want to say to me about my walk with you?" Wait in silence as the Holy Spirit reveals truth to you.

Questions to Ask the Lord

1. What things am I most focusing on?

2. Are any of these things receiving too much of my attention?

3. Ask the Lord to give you any questions he wants you to ask him...

Today, go somewhere where children are playing or simply think back to times you have interacted with children. Ask God to give you the heart of a child as you spend time with him. Ask God to teach you and speak to you through the children.

DAY TWENTY

GROWING DEEP ROOTS

One day Jesus was telling his disciples what to do when God spoke to them through an allegory of a seed, its soil, and its roots. "Those on the rock are the ones who receive the word with joy when they hear it, but they have no root. They believe for a while, but in the time of testing they fall away." He went on to describe three things in particular that keep the word of God from taking root in our lives: worries, riches, and pleasures. (Luke 8:13-14)

Claud Crosby was a normal college student in Richmond, Virginia. Claud learned the truth of Luke 8:14. The devil tried to steal the seed of God's word that had been planted by attacking him with doubt and worry. Not more than half an hour after God spoke to him, the devil did as well: "God didn't really speak to you back there." Claud found himself caught up in a cloud of worry and confusion.

It all started one day when, out of the blue, God spoke to him and said, "Go to Philadelphia and be discipled." That word from the Lord flew in the face of a lot of expectations and life patterns.

"Out of all the believers I knew," Claud said, "only one friend said, 'you're in God's will.' All the others said, 'God wouldn't have you quit school.' I told my two closest friends, a couple of the most passionate believers I know, that I had to follow God and leave. They said they didn't believe that I cared about them. Both have since fallen away from the Lord."

When God said, "Go," Claud was faced with a number of decisions. He loved his BMX bike, but knew that it had become an idol which he needed to lay down.

Later, another issue, money, was introduced. Well-meaning family members came to him and said, "Your needs are being met where you are. How are you going to provide for them in Philadelphia?"

Two years later, Claud had grown in his faith by leaps and bounds. He had been discipled in a radical faith and had ministered to addicts and street people, helping dozens of them to find their way out of hopelessness. Truly, the word of the Lord was a precious and fragile thing to Claud. Because he was a good steward, God's relational roots grew deep in him.

The discovery that it is possible to converse with God can come as a gradual dawning or a crashing revelation. Either way, it can be life-changing. The proof is in the pudding. Your life will change if you choose to actually hold regular conversations with God – conversations that cause you to deepen and make more personal your relationship with him.

Roots

Any relationship needs time to grow roots. In fact, Jesus used this illustration of roots to describe our response to his invitation to converse with him. To understand his point, we need to grapple with what he means when he uses the term "word." The most basic unit of meaning in a conversation is a single word. The word "Go!" has been a life-altering word that God has uttered to his followers ever since Abraham.

Taken collectively, a piece of conversation, maybe a phrase, sentence, or even a paragraph can be thought of as a "word." This terminology can get confusing. Someone may say that they received a "word" from the Lord, when in fact they actually received several sentences. That is the broad meaning that Jesus assigns it in Luke 8:11. In his parable, the "word," as represented by a seed, is a message, a God-generated bit of communication received by men as thoughts that are then packaged in words.

Relational roots, like plant roots, grow slowly and imperceptibly over time. They respond to watering, but it is the quality of the soil that impacts them most.

The soil represents our attitude. If we want to see our relationship with the Lord grow, we need an attitude of eagerness. We need to actively seek to converse with him, or to just hang out in his presence. This past year, I decided to grow tomatoes, but I didn't plow the tough, Georgia clay deeply enough. The tomato plants grew rapidly, and then one day their leaves began to turn yellow. The soil was too shallow; their roots couldn't go deeper.

That's how it is with our conversations with God. If our attitude begins to sag and we don't make time for him, then our relationship will suffer. If we want to experience the riches of the deep, personal relationship, we will maintain an attitude of eagerness to know him and be with him over time. When he speaks, we will actively listen, applying his word to our lives. And when we go through dry spells, we won't walk away from the relationship – every relationship has its dry spells. Remember, God says, "You will seek me and find me when you seek me with all your heart." Only a whole-hearted seeking will see you through the dry times.

If you have struggled to maintain long-lasting friendships, then it's likely you'll also struggle with consistency in your relationship with Christ. Each day that dawns presents a new opportunity to "seek the Lord, while he may be found."

Scripture Meditation

Spend a minute or more just thinking about the following

passage: "The seed is the word of God. Those along the path are the ones who hear, and then the devil comes and takes away the word from their hearts." (Luke 8:11-12a)

Pray

"Heavenly Father, I don't want to be one of those who hears the word but forgets and fails to follow through. I want to be one who is a faithful doer of the word. Show me what needs to change in my life so that the roots of our relationship can grow deep." Wait in silence as the Holy Spirit reveals truth to you.

Questions to Ask the Lord

1. Are there any past experiences in my life, any hurts in particular that have led me to believe that it's not safe to trust people? What are they?

2. Are there any relationships in my past that have made it difficult for me to be faithful communicating either with friends or with you, Lord? If so, would you show them to me?

3. Will you show me what I need to do to put those relational difficulties behind me?

4. What can I do now to move toward a deeper-rooted walk with you?

What does abundant life look like to you? God has amazing plans and purposes for his people. Spend some time seeking God about the abundant life. What does it mean for you today?

DAY TWENTY—ONE

OVERCOMING OBSTACLES: WORRIES

Almost a week before leaving, Christy McGraw wrote to tell me that she was backing out of my 2003 missions trip to England. I asked her if God had told her not to go and she said, "My grandmother needs me and I'm worried about getting the money in."

So I asked her, "Pray about it over the weekend."

The next week she answered, "Okay, I guess I'm supposed to go."

Amazingly, the rest of the money she needed came in during the next week. After the trip, she wrote the following:

"God's love is so important to our life, but sometimes we don't think we deserve it. God sent me to England to heal my broken heart and to help me realize I am worthy of his GREAT Love. I have always felt a sense of worthlessness in my life. I never felt I was worthy of anything from friends to family and even God's love. But all that changed August 2nd.

As a team, we were having a time of prayer and worship where Mary Lou (a team leader) was going to pray for boldness for each of us. When she got to me and touched me, I just started to sob. God had let Mary Lou know some things about me. I had let Satan enter my mind and tell me how worthless I was and how I didn't deserve love. This had been happening a long time.

We prayed against this feeling of worthlessness and as we prayed I felt something released from around my heart. I felt free from this burden of worthlessness; Satan no longer had a hold of my mind. God loves me so very much–more than I could ever imagine! God took all those lies and threw them away and in one touch healed my heart and made it whole!

After this powerful experience with God, I learned even more about just how loving our Father is and how extraordinary Christ is. It took me leaving everything I held near to my heart—my family, friends, and church—for God to show me how magnificent he really is. I praise him for the opportunity to go on this trip and I praise him for changing my life!"

Why We Worry

Even after the last several weeks of going through this devotional, even if you've discovered that God wants to communicate with you personally and have begun to hear his voice, the devil is not sweating. He knows how to use our short attention spans and tendency to worry to rob us of the word of the Lord. To make conversation with God a lifestyle, we have to do battle with our enemy and with our own nature.

Perhaps you're one who struggles with a "Martha" spirit, a frequent wringing of your hands in worry. You're conscientious—concerned about getting stuff done. As a consequence, the clock ticks by and you find yourself fretting.

Perhaps you care so deeply that things be done well that sometimes your concern becomes a worry and crowds out your compassion for people. How do you find balance?

If we are to grow in our ability to focus our attention on God as we communicate with him, we have to address the issue of worry. We worry because we doubt that something we want to happen, something that we may feel responsible to help make happen, is actually never going to come to pass. We may find ourselves hearing God say something one moment, only to find worries about a relational conflict or an upcoming test filling our minds and crowding out what God has said to us. It could even be something as abstract and out of our control as the prospects for world peace.

Worries introduce the lie that God either doesn't care or that he lacks power. They are rooted in the conclusion that we are not God's children, adopted into his family, but are in fact more like orphans with no one to look out for us.

By definition, worries are just thoughts. They fill the mind, take up space, and prevent at least for a time, the possibility of kingdom thinking. It's impossible to simultaneously entertain a worry and to trust God. James 1:8 calls such a person who does this "double-minded." James observes that because they lack conviction, they are unstable.

God wants to provide for our needs, but to receive his provision we have to trust him. Worrying deprives us of that ability to trust. It calls our adoption into question. Worrying takes the responsibility of providing for our needs out of our heavenly Father's hands, where they belong, and places them into our own. When we worry, we assume ownership of the problem, figuring that if it's going to be resolved, then it's up to us.

There's a difference between worries and concerns. A concern stems from taking responsibility for the completion of a task. It's normal when one has a responsibility to think about the way in which it will be accomplished. Just because details pop into one's mind doesn't mean they are from the devil. But when those concerns are compulsively and repetitively recycled through one's brain, they turn into worries – thoughts which crowd out the word of the Lord through the constant murmur of unfulfilled details.

It isn't enough to decide to stop worrying. That only addresses the symptom of the real root. For example, the mere thought, "I am an orphan. I am responsible for my own provision," may turn into an inability to trust God. Until that lie has been addressed and exchanged for the truth, "God loves me and has promised to care for me," worry is going to be our inevitable companion, filling our minds when it is most crucial that they be fixed on the Lord.

Apply It

Let me encourage you to meditate on what the Bible says about worry: "Do not worry about your life, what you will eat; or about your body, what you will wear...who of you by worrying can add a single hour to his life?" (Luke 12:22,25)

"Do not worry about tomorrow, for tomorrow will worry about itself. Each day has enough trouble of its own." (Matthew 6:34)

"Do not be anxious about anything, but in everything...present your requests to God." (Philippians 4:6)

Scripture Meditation

Spend a minute or more just thinking about the following passage: "The seed that fell among thorns stands for those who hear, but as they go on their way they are choked by life's worries, riches and pleasures, and they do not mature...Therefore consider carefully how you listen." (Luke 8:14, 18)

Pray

"Heavenly Father, it's natural for people to worry. But I want to trust you and live by your Spirit. Is this passage true for me in the area of worry? Have I let anxiety come between you and me? What do you want to say to me about worry?" Wait in silence as the Holy Spirit reveals truth to you.

Questions to Ask the Lord

Ask the Lord the questions below. Write down your impression of what he may be saying.

1. What areas of my life am I most concerned about? Why?

2. Do I trust you with all these areas? Which ones do I not trust you in?

3. What does that reveal about what I believe of your power?

4. What does it reveal about what I believe of your love for me?

5. What is the truth about those two things?

6. What should I do next time I start to worry?

Lord, help me to know that I don't need to worry. Break down barriers in my life so that I can trust you. Reveal to me those things I fear that cause me to worry.

DAY TWENTY—TWO

OVERCOMING OBSTACLES: RICHES

*W*hen Peri Forister heard God call her to come work with us at Adventures In Missions, life began to get complicated. As a single woman with her budgetary needs already limited, she still had to raise financial support.

She wasn't excited about the prospect of sharing her need with her family and friends, so she prayed about it. Then it got worse. God said to give away all the money that she had saved up in her life.

Forister had worked a variety of jobs to save over $3,000. Her savings represented a lot of hard work. To think of parting with it was distressing; but she knew that God had said to do it and she was determined to obey him. So, one day she got out her checkbook and pen.

Forister had a list of charities and people who needed help. Tears spilled down her face as one by one she began to write the checks. Eventually she had drawn the account down to zero. She set aside the checkbook completely exhausted. While she was glad to be able to help them, it wasn't easy to empty her checking account.

Having given away all her money, Forister was completely dependent on the Lord, which was exactly what he wanted. Now the pledges of financial support began to fly at her from all over! She was overwhelmed by how quickly the support came in. Within a month, she had all the pledges she needed and was able to start her missionary work. Just as she had proven herself trustworthy with the Lord's word, he had proven himself trustworthy to her.

Maybe in your struggle to grow in your conversational relationship with God you don't worry that much—the enemy has many other weapons in his arsenal. Some of these include weapons like the temptation to rely on yourself when you have been blessed with an abundance of resources.

It could even be that you've never struggled with money. Perhaps you've always had a good head on your shoulders about it; you've understood God's provision, and you've tried to be a good steward of his resources. Most of us in America don't need to ask the Lord for our daily bread—it's just always there.

A Mixed Blessing

In many ways, having money can be a mixed blessing. On the one hand, it's nice to know that your physical needs are taken care of. On the other, it takes away the blessing of praying, "Give us this day our daily bread," and actually watching God answer the prayer. Dependence on God is a wonderful thing. It brings you closer to him and enhances your partnership with him.

God is very interested in being trusted. He bet the farm on the notion that partnership with men would work. That's why he wants us to depend on him. When we do things in his power, the partnership is working. But when we don't, therein lies the real problem of riches—they take away the necessity of trusting God. With personal needs met, we don't have to depend on God. We may talk to him, but it's easy to say, "You go your way, and I'll go mine."

The Scriptures are full of warnings against the dangers of wealth—it whispers the lie, "You really don't need God; why bother collaborating with him when you can enjoy life?"

Consider these passages:

• "Now listen, you rich people, weep and wail because of the misery that is coming upon you. Your wealth has rotted...your gold and silver are corroded." (James 5:1-3)
• "People who want to get rich fall into temptation and a trap and into many foolish and harmful desires that plunge men into ruin and destruction." (1 Timothy 6:9)
• "No servant can serve two masters...You cannot serve both God and Money." (Luke 16:13)
• "How hard it is for the rich to enter the kingdom of God." (Luke18: 24)
• "Do not store up for yourselves treasures on earth, where moth and rust destroy." (Matthew 6:19)

All of these passages point to the concept that it's not riches themselves that are the problem—it's our attitude toward them. The issue is: can we remain dependent on God and exercise good stewardship when we have been entrusted with wealth? Or, will we begin to ignore his costly directives when they conflict with our own desires?

Scripture Meditation

Spend a minute or more just thinking about the following passage: "The seed that fell among thorns stands for those who hear, but as they go on their way they are choked by life's worries, riches and pleasures, and they do not mature...Therefore consider carefully how you listen." (Luke 8:14, 18)

Pray

"Lord, do you want to talk with me about money? Has my attitude toward money honored you? What do you want to teach me about this passage?" Wait in silence as the Holy Spirit reveals truth to you.

Questions to Ask the Lord

1. Am I satisfied with my financial status right now? Do I truly depend on you?

2. Do I have an attitude of dependence on your provision for me? Show me my heart.

3. What do you think about my generosity? My spirit of gratitude?

4. What does my attitude toward my own finances reveal about what I believe about you?

5. How, specifically, can I grow in this area?

DAY TWENTY—THREE

OVERCOMING OBSTACLES: PLEASURES

*I*t may be an earth-shattering revelation to those who know me, but I do struggle with sin issues on a regular basis. One particular area comes to mind where I periodically get out of balance.

All my life I've loved sports. Growing up in Missouri, I used to listen to the St. Louis Cardinals baseball games on a little red radio with an earpiece during the summer. I also watched the Missouri Tiger football and basketball games with my father.

As an adult, I've become a Washington Redskins fan. Now don't roll your eyes and think, "I can see where this is going—sports are bad, right?" That's not my conclusion here. But let me tell you about the tension in which I live. At best, I skate close to the edge. For example, everyday during off-season, I check to see what moves the Redskins management has made. I know all the players and their strengths. I keep abreast of trade talks. At times as I'm dropping off to sleep, thoughts of how the team is going to do swim through my head. On game days I'm a little more excited.

The problem is that there are times when I want to go pray and connect with God and those football thoughts get in the way. At times it obstructs my conversation with God. I must not allow my interest in football to become an idol—God must come first.

This past week, the Holy Spirit told me to rein it in by "fasting" from football for two weeks. I don't believe God is a spoilsport who wants to deprive me of things that add spice to my life. But I recognize that he's a jealous God and I'm treading on thin ice if I devote more energy to anything other than him.

If you have a wonderful zest for life that leads you to sometimes obsess over interests or hobbies, then this may be where you'll struggle the most as you talk to God. It's great that the Lord has built you in such a way that you're pulled in the direction of excitement and adventure, but recognize that it can distract you.

If you have a keen sense of fun, you probably have a lot of good times with your friends because people are attracted to you. This motivation you have is a wonderful gift. The world is too serious and goodness knows, we need levity in our lives. At the same time, you've probably seen the potential that exists for things to get out of balance in your walk with God. The Bible warns us that pleasures can crowd out the word of God in our lives.

People who are distracted by thoughts about their favorite sports team, video game, movie, or even by relationships, tend to have this struggle. They sit down to pray, God speaks, conviction comes, and then competing thoughts come flooding in. Pleasurable activities are sometimes called "diversions," because they can certainly divert us from the path of listening and obedience.

Pleasures can be a subset of the sin of idolatry. God's first commandment is that we make him #1 in our lives. We are to love him with all our heart, mind, and strength. He was so earnest about this that his second commandment spells out how to avoid diluting our love for him through idolatry.

The things that could potentially give us pleasure are innumerable. Look at the number of specialty magazines on the racks in a bookstore: bodybuilding, sewing, gardening, football, video games, music, fashion;

the list goes on and on. People can lose themselves in any number of diversions. Often, because the activity itself brings a sense of pleasure, it's only natural to want to learn more about it. The more you learn, the greater your interest. One fact learned leads to another until the area of casual interest turns into a hobby. Ultimately, the hobby can turn into an obsession and that, in turn, can become an addiction. Even at the casual interest stage, it is possible to crowd out thoughts of God, both while engaged in the actual activity, and then afterwards, while thinking about it. In and of themselves these pleasures may not be wrong, but they become harmful to your soul when the space in your mind that normally would be filled with God-thoughts is filled by other thoughts.

Of course, this is a gray area. God wants us to enjoy life. He wants us to delight in his many-splendored creation. But he also wants to find that place of intimacy in our lives. Like a spurned spouse, he feels it when our heart beats after other things more than after him. Pleasures become a problem when they obstruct our view of God.

Here are a few passages to consider on the subject:

• "People will be lovers of themselves, lovers of money...lovers of pleasure, rather than lovers of God...Have nothing to do with them." (2 Timothy 3:1-5)
• "The widow who lives for pleasure is dead even while she lives." (1 Timothy 5:6)
• "He who loves pleasure will become poor." (Proverbs 21:17)
• "Their idea of pleasure is to carouse in broad daylight. They are blots and blemishes, reveling in their pleasures..." (2 Peter 2:13)

Scripture Meditation

Spend a moment just thinking about the following passage: "The seed that fell among thorns stands for those who hear, but as they go on their way they are choked by life's worries, riches and pleasures, and they do not mature...Therefore consider carefully how you listen." (Luke 8:14,18)

Pray

"Lord, you gain pleasure from my enjoyment of the things you've made, yet you are the only one who can fulfill my deepest desires. It's so easy for me to fall into idolatry and seek other things than you. I need to have balance here, Father. What do you want to say to me about pleasures?" Wait in silence as the Holy Spirit reveals truth to you.

Questions to Ask the Lord

1. What are my favorite hobbies and pleasures?

2. Are any of these taking up too much of my time, money, energy or attention?

3. Are any of them infringing on my key relationships in my family, at work or with you?

4. What do you want to say to me about this, Lord?

5. What would you have me do?

DAY TWENTY—FOUR

PERSEVERING THROUGH PAIN

*L*ouise Perrotta's challenging book, *All You Really Need to Know About Prayer You Can Learn From the Poor*, recounts stories of some who have had to wrestle with the issue of pain.*

Sister Regina is one of them. She's a nun who cares for the downcast of Jamaica. When she asks the poor to whom she ministers, "What do you have to offer the Lord?" she gets a variety of answers:

"I Have Eviction."

Marlene Allen used to offer to the Lord as her daily prayer the eviction threats she kept receiving for her landlady. Not that Marlene's shack was a castle. In fact, it was the second worst living situation I've seen in all these years of going in and out of poor houses. Rotten wood, rusted zinc, rats everywhere, an overflowing pit toilet, a cramped room maybe three by five—these are the conditions in which Marlene was struggling to raise four children, one of them severely retarded.

"I Have A Plastic Tent."

Althea Hook and her four children were burned out of their last house and now live in a make-shift shelter with no more protection from the elements than four plastic sides and a plastic roof. "How do you talk to the Lord about this problem, Althea?" I asked her. Very simply she replied, "I tell him, Lord help me get a job and earn something for my children and I. There's nowhere to live. This plastic tent is terrible when rain comes; it wets up." Althea cried here, and I cried later in my own prayers because she went on to say: "Sometimes I give up. I tell the Lord, 'When my children cry and have nothing to eat... Lord, before you suffer them more, take them back.'"

Jesus wants more than the sporadic communication that is our habit. He wants more than the monologues we are prone to pray. He wants us to be careful how we listen. He tells us to hear the word of God, retain it, and persevere. He said, "But the seed on good soil stands for those with a noble and good heart, who hear the word, retain it, and by persevering produce a crop."

Luke 8:14 points to worries, riches, and pleasures as among the greatest obstacles to retaining God's word—it is through persevering that we bear fruit. The concept of persevering implies overcoming pain in various forms. As long as things are going well in your life, listening for God's voice may be easy enough. When all other obstacles that the devil throws your way fail, he resorts to pain. Conversely, if you have proven yourself trustworthy to God, he may trust you with pain. How will you do in tough times? This is the age-old bet that Satan makes with God, the best example of which we see in the book of Job. It goes like this: "I'll bet your servant is just in it for the good times, let's see how he does with a little pain in his life."

There may be some who at this point would say to me, "Yeah, that's easy for you to say, you've never gone through what's happened to me... you don't understand my pain." But I have an answer.

You're right. It's true. Yet while our family is exceedingly blessed, we have also known pain of our own. In particular, my youngest daughter has experienced more pain than anyone should ever have to go through. When she was young, she had a chronic infection in her ears that was extremely painful, making it hard for her to hear. In addition to her physical pain, she struggled just to understand what people were saying.

When she was a little older, we discovered that her palate wasn't fully formed. Issues of memory and learning became more apparent. Despite numerous surgeries, she has not been able to articulate words as most people do. Recently, she's been having seizures. She has been labeled by professionals and isolated from her peers. She has struggled with what it means to be different. Loneliness is her frequent companion. Every week my wife takes her an hour away to see specialists. And we as parents carry the burdens of crushed hopes while trying to meet all the special needs.

I don't have any answers for her when I see her heart broken because other people have friends and she doesn't. When she looks at me with eyes that say, "Daddy, it's not fair," I don't have answers for her. It's not fair! Why is it that some people never seem to catch a break? All I know is that it can send them to Jesus' feet faster than other people. That's why he said, "Blessed are the poor in spirit." The brokenhearted need Jesus more than the rest of us.

Because it's not fair that my daughter—or anyone else—should be saddled with so much pain. Therefore, we have a choice. We can either shake our fists at an all-powerful God who seemingly put us in this mess, or we can choose to trust and worship him, knowing that somehow he will redeem it.

As hard as it is to say it, we don't have any other choice. All of us who have experienced pain like my daughter would seem to have a right to be angry at God and to allow that anger to crystallize into bitterness. But we can't go there—our Father God is the author of all life. Somehow in the midst of the pain, even through tears, we have to look to the "Father of lights" who, the Bible tells us, gives us good and perfect gifts. We have to trust him. As we trust him, he does answer us; and if that answer doesn't stop our pain, at least it redeems it. Leah has a strong faith and trusts in God with her whole heart.

All of your life, you'll have opportunities to have a vindictive spirit when bad and painful things happen, and to turn and blame God. But if you have a testimony of patience and long-suffering in the face of pain, you will not only dwell in that peace, but also show people the characteristics of Jesus. The potential exists for God's word to dwell richly within you.

Scripture Meditation

Spend a minute or more just thinking about the following passage: "I consider that our present sufferings are not worth comparing with the glory that will be revealed in us." (Romans 8:18)

Pray

"Heavenly Father, this is such a hard passage to read when I'm hurting. Yet you wrote it to help in our suffering. Please help me to understand it now, the way you intended, and to better understand you. What do you want to say to me about this passage?" Wait in silence as the Holy Spirit reveals truth to you.

Questions to Ask the Lord

1. Have I expected that you, because of your goodness, power and love, would keep your children from significant pain?

2. Do I have any anger towards you or others, Lord, because of pain?

3. What are some Scriptures you've written for us about pain?

4. So, what is the truth about pain, Lord?

5. What can I do with it? What should be my response to it?

HELPING OTHERS TO HEAR GOD

After discovering the marvelous secret that God wants to communicate with me on a regular basis, one of my first responses was to think, "I've got to share this with my children."

At that point, they were young—all of them under the age of nine. In the morning, the four oldest and I knelt in front of the living room couch.

"If we go to God and ask him questions, I've discovered that he wants to answer us. He loves you and wants to talk to you like I'm talking to you now."

"You mean that he'll talk to us out loud?" one of them said. "Well, he might, but he usually talks to us in our minds in a way that only we can hear."

"What does that sound like?"

"It sounds like a thought. So pay attention to the thoughts you have. Some might be God whispering to you." Then we all bowed our heads and began to pray. Every now and then I'd prompt them with another question. "First, let's make sure that we haven't hurt God's feelings by doing things we know are wrong. So, pray like this: "God, would you show me anything I've done that I need to confess to you?"

After a time of silence, I asked them, "Did the Lord show you anything?"

"Yes," they all replied. "Well, then go ahead and ask God's forgiveness for it now."

"Lord, forgive me for pulling Emily's hair," one said. Another spoke, "God, I'm sorry for having a bad attitude."

This continued for a while—they were getting it—God was talking to them! After this, I continued to guide them in listening prayer, posing questions for them to ask God. It was wonderful to see their lack of inhibition in communicating with the Father. We continued to meet together until I became confident that they were able to practice listening prayer on their own.

Two thoughts came to me as I reflected on the experience. First, listening prayer comes naturally for children—perhaps they have less stuff that gets in the way. Second, I was surprised by how much unconfessed sin they had. I couldn't help thinking, "If they didn't have this opportunity, then they'd be dragging all those sins and habits around."

Helping Others

People need help in getting to know the Lord personally. While their lack of experience may protect them from a cynical attitude, new believers need to be guided along the path toward a conversational relationship with the Father. Left to their own devices, my children would not have encountered him. But with a little help, they readily found their way to his side.

Many Christians would readily admit that they have never heard God speak. Yet in our desire to help them, it is possible to inadvertently cause them to fall victim to a trap. In the great open expanse of our mind, myriad thoughts rush to and fro; many voices cry out for attention. Remember, most of these thoughts or voices come from our daily activity—the things we have seen and heard. In the midst of all this noise, God's still, small voice speaks to us. When someone is unpracticed in listening to him, he or she we will frequently mistake their own thoughts for his.

It's helpful to explain to your protégé that God did

not make automatons, people who just do what he tells them to do. He gave us free will so that we might seek him of our own volition. Were we robots, he would simply dictate a to-do list in prayer to us every morning. The fact is, he doesn't do this and, therefore, we should not expect that he will tell us what to do simply because we asked. While we make clear our availability and expectancy, we also recognize that he has given us our general marching orders. Often he chooses to speak to us not before, but in the midst of the battle.

Scripture Meditation

Spend a minute or more just thinking about the following passage: "And the things you have heard me say in the presence of many witnesses entrust to reliable men who will also be qualified to teach others." (2 Timothy 2:2)

Pray

"Lord, how is this verse true for me? Are there reliable men whom I can trust? How can I equip them to teach others? What do you want to say to me about this passage?" Wait in silence as the Holy Spirit reveals truth to you.

Questions to Ask the Lord

1. Whom do you want me to disciple in hearing your voice?

2. Do I have a track record of failing to look for your rhema word? How can I grow in this?

3. Am I overly concerned with my own dignity? Is there anything I need to do to grow in humility?

4. What cautions do I particularly need to observe?

DAY TWENTY—SIX

WHAT'S NEXT?

*I*f God has spoken to you during this last month and you're like me, you'll want to find ways to continue listening for his voice as you go forward from here. How can you do that? Here are a few ideas:

Fight Your Enemy

First, recognize the principle of shallow roots in Luke 8. Your sworn enemy, the devil, loves the tactic of allowing you to taste the abundant life Jesus promised and then, over time, to call its validity into question. "Did the Lord really speak to you?" he asks sarcastically.

That is another reason why journaling is helpful. One way to fight your enemy is to review what God has said. If the Lord gave you a promise, then boldly pray it back to him: "Lord, I thank you that you promised me: _____. I claim that promise today in Jesus' name and ask that you activate it in my life. I renounce the lies of the enemy and stand on the truth of your word."

Continue Your Discipline

Second, continue in your discipline of setting aside uninterrupted time to be with God. Remember, he is a jealous God. He doesn't want to compete for your attention. When you meet with the Lord, ask him your own questions and take the time to patiently wait for his response.

Share It

Third, recognize that one of the best ways to grow is to share what God has shown you with others. Ask the Lord to show you who he would like to help you along this path.

Practice With Others

Listening prayer is not an activity to be practiced exclusively on your own. When you're in a team that needs direction from the Lord, one of the best things you can do is to ask him questions together. Bring something to write on as you pray and wait on him.

Scripture Meditation

Keep up the practice of meditating on the Scripture.

Ask the Lord

Remember to keep asking the Lord questions and waiting for his response. He enjoys conversation with you!

Accountability

If you haven't done so yet, it's time to get a partner to look at the things you hear God saying to you. Find a mature, godly friend whom you trust and ask them to look over your journal and give you feedback.

RECOMMENDED READING

Experiencing God, Henry Blackaby

A very popular workbook that helps you grasp the concept that "God is at work in the world and we just need to join him in what he is doing."

When God Speaks, Henry & Richard Blackaby

A workbook that helps you understand why God wants to communicate with us and how he does so.

Surprised by the Power of the Spirit, Jack Deere

An evangelical's apologetic for the notion that God's miraculous works have not ceased in our day and age.

Surprised by the Voice of God, Jack Deere

Deere goes further down the prophetic road.

Listening Prayer, Leanne Payne

Explains the various ways in which we can listen for God's voice and step out in ministry at his behest.

Hearing God, Peter Lord

The original bestseller that demolishes our notions that God is restricted to speaking through the Bible.

Communion with God, Mark Virkler

A thorough workbook for those who want to continue to appropriate what the Lord has said about talking to us.

Hearing God, Dallas Willard

The definitive exegesis of the theological concept that the Holy Spirit speaks to us in multiple ways.

The Voice of God, Cindy Jacobs

For those who want to explore the dimensions of the prophetic gift, this book outlines how it operates and how to grow in it.

Intercession, Joy Dawson

If you feel the Lord calling you to a deeper walk of prayer, this book will provide helpful direction.

The Hour that Changes the World, Dick Eastman

Outlines a practical system for prayer

Rees Howells, Intercessor, Norman Grubbs

The biography of an intercessor who gradually proved his faithfulness to the Lord, and then watched as God entrusted him with a ministry that impacted the world.

ABOUT THE AUTHOR

Seth Barnes is the founder and director of Adventures In Missions in Gainesville, Georgia.

Since 1989, more than 100,000 people have gone on mission projects through Adventures in Missions.

Adventures' objective is to raise up a generation of radically committed disciples of Jesus Christ. Its ministry strongly emphasizes discipleship and prayer. Those going on projects are taught how to use listening prayer to seek the Holy Spirit's guidance in ministry. They come away changed.

Seth and his wife Karen have five children, two sons-in-law, and one grandson (so far!). They live in Gainesville, Georgia with their youngest daughter, one dog, two cats, and whatever missionaries are visiting and living in their basement. Seth and Karen are graduates of Wheaton College. They served as missionaries in Indonesia and the Dominican Republic.

Seth went on his first mission project in the summer of his junior year in high school. That trip to Huehuetenango, Guatemala, changed his life. He saw poverty and hopelessness that he'd never imagined before. At the same time, he saw that he could do something about it. Convicted by God's heart for the poor and oppressed in Isaiah 58, Seth determined to commit his life to helping others understand that they can make a difference.

Please visit Adventures in Missions' website at:
WWW.ADVENTURES.ORG

"If you spend yourselves in behalf of the hungry

and satisfy the needs of the oppressed,

then your light will rise in the darkness,

and your night will become like the noonday..."

Isaiah 58:10

SETH BARNES

Made in the USA
Las Vegas, NV
12 April 2024

88593536R00100